Not Allergic to Happiness, Just Gluten!

How to Love Your Life With a Food Allergy or Celiac Disease

Liz Bogens

Not Allergic to Happiness, Just Gluten! How to Love Your Life With a Food Allergy or Celiac Disease

Copyright © 2023 by Liz Bogens

All rights reserved.

First Edition

Paperback ISBN: 979-8-375-75046-0
Hardback ISBN: 979-8-376-06541-9

Editor: Sam Wright
Cover Design: Kate Pavlou

Printed in: see last page

Information according to German law, § 5 TMG:
Liz Bogens is represented by
Sabrina M. Hanrath
Oesternkamp 18
D-33415 Verl, Germany
liz.bogens@gmail.com

For Kevin.
You were with me on this journey from the start.
I couldn't have asked for a better partner at my side.

And for my mom.
Thank you for making me feel included
at the dinner table and at family reunions.

AUTHOR'S NOTE

Dear Reader,

I hope this book will help you on your path to happiness. I have poured much love and energy into this book and can only hope you feel it while reading these pages.

Know that you are not alone with your struggles. I believe that if we don't give up on happiness and keep fighting for it, it will come (back) eventually.

I have consciously chosen to keep this book as light and fun as possible, even though (or perhaps because) the underlying topic can feel heavy. Because for me, it's a happy book! I'm truly excited to share this with you.

Yours gluten-freely,
Liz

CONTENTS

Introduction 1

Resilience 5

Understand Your Dietary Restrictions 7

Pillar 1: Acceptance 17

    Feelings and What to Do About Them 20

    True Gamechanger: Expectation Management 24

    My Truths (Overview) 46

    Pain Points, Underlying Needs, and Solutions 49

    Life Hacks for Your Gluten-Free Lifestyle 57

Pillar 2: Support Network 69

    Yourself 70

    Friends and Family 72

    Gluten-Free Community 74

    Professionals 77

    Dealing with Non-Supportive People 80

    Life Hacks: Clapping Back 83

Pillar 3: The Right Mindset 95

    Take Back Your Power 96

    Healthy Optimism and Being Solution-Driven 103

    Confidence and Boundaries 105

    Perspective and Gratitude 108

    Friendly Thoughts 112

    Humor 124

    Dealing with Stress 125

    Life Hacks: Thinking in the Right Direction 127

Final Thoughts 131

References 134

Not Allergic to Happiness, Just Gluten!

How to Love Your Life With a Food Allergy or Celiac Disease

INTRODUCTION

You live a somewhat normal life, and then it happens: you're diagnosed with celiac disease, gluten intolerance, or a food allergy. If you picked up this book, chances are that you or a loved one has it. They are more common than you might think: it is estimated that 5% of adults suffer from allergies, which are predicted to rise even further. Gluten, lactose, fructose, nuts, eggs, soy, or fish are some of the most common food groups.

At 26, I was diagnosed with gluten intolerance and a high likelihood of having celiac disease. Celiac disease is an autoimmune disease where eating gluten can cause harm to the small intestine. I am not alone: estimations say that about 1% of the world population suffers from celiac disease.

Transitioning into the gluten-free lifestyle, I was somewhat naïve about how big the impact on me would be. It's far more than not eating gluten. Anyone with a food allergy or food intolerance knows what I'm talking about.

This change affected my body, mind, and soul. I quickly learned that "only" eating according to my new dietary restrictions (e.g., gluten-free) also affects nearly every aspect of my life. I compare it to a ripple effect.

Being restricted in my diet also affects social occasions. I could no longer join them as freely as I would have liked to. I realized that food and social interactions are often intertwined. Plus the additional frustration that I actually *would* like to eat what everyone else is eating, not just to feel included but also simply because I love pizza. Often, I need to let people know why and what I cannot eat, a discussion I didn't need to have before.

Initially, this was difficult because I had yet to process my emotions. I didn't enjoy talking about it. Also, I needed time to understand what I could or couldn't eat.

I have experienced pleasant and painful reactions to my dietary "demands." At first, I found it difficult to relax around situations in which food was involved. Sometimes, I even forget about my new allergy, only to remember it again and check my plate to see if everything is edible. Even when I sleep, I sometimes dream of being hungry and walking around the cafeteria, only to realize there is nothing there without gluten. Come to think of it, I have even experienced that in real life!

I watched everyone choose from a huge menu while I was stuck with choosing from two gluten-free options if any. I felt somewhat betrayed by my comfort food, now forbidden to eat. Being a foodie and relying on food as a source of joy, this new diagnosis was hard on me.

It didn't feel like I was only allergic to gluten. It felt like I was also now allergic to happiness. I felt like I was tapping around in the dark, trying to find the light switch. I wondered if a light switch even existed.

To make matters worse, I could not find the advice I needed. Countless books and resources discuss what to eat or details of the medical condition I had. There were rules to follow and countless recipes, both online and offline. I have also encountered material where authors complained or let off steam about how difficult life has become.

But what about overcoming the mental struggles and challenges faced every day? Psychologically speaking, a food allergy has the potential to impact the diagnosed person quite a lot. It impacted me and my life to a large extent, especially mentally. I spoke to others in similar situations and got the same feedback from them.

I couldn't find the book I was looking for: a positive, heartfelt book that would take me by the hand and lovingly help me heal. So, I wrote my own book. I have been doing extensive research specifically on this topic and building on the years before my diagnosis when I was interested in psychology and mental health as a hobby. My mission was clear: I needed to find real-life solutions that work. It took a while, but I found them with great success.

I want to share my key insights with you. Like me back then, you or a loved one may struggle to get helpful (mental health) advice on this challenging topic. I hope this book supports you in finding joy again and creating your own happiness, no matter the circumstances.

I've written down the revelations I've had and lessons I've learned along the way that led me to my success: being at peace, being genuinely happy, and loving my life, despite the inconveniences I've been struggling with.

My examples are based on gluten sensitivity/intolerance and celiac disease scenarios, but the advice can also be applied to other food allergies/intolerances. Even those without a food allergy/intolerance can find many key insights to a joyful life. In the following, I will use the term food *allergies*, but please know that food *intolerances* and *sensitivities* are also included when I do.

In this book, I aim to tell it like it is and offer practical advice that works. The main message of this book is not "there are so many gluten-free options, you'll be fine, just think positive." We will explore real feelings, real problems, and real reactions. We must face the truth and manage our best response to the situation. Don't worry, there will be a happy ending. But a realistic one that is long-lasting and sustainable.

So, without further ado, I invite you into the arena. Let's fight for a joyful life and happiness. No more tapping around in the dark. Let's turn on the lights.

RESILIENCE

At its core, resilience is about making it through challenges that may arise and recovering from them quickly. It's about bouncing back. If we look at these new dietary restrictions as a challenge, resilience may help in "recovering" from this challenge.

Contrary to common belief, resilience is not just something you must be born with. It can be learned and perfected continuously throughout life.

With this book, I want to help you become resilient. I have put together all the best practices that have worked for me and that I found helpful on my journey to happiness and resilience.

Building on my own experiences and considering two resilience models (Kenneth Ginsburg's "7 C's" and Ursula Nuber's seven pillars of resilience), I have created my pillars for food allergy resilience.

These three pillars are the foundation of being resilient despite having a food allergy:

1: Acceptance
2: Support Network
3: The Right Mindset

I will address each of these pillars separately and share what I have learned about each of them. Still, you will find traces of them all throughout the book because these pillars can overlap at times.

Also, you do not need to work on one pillar until you've mastered it to move on to a different pillar. This is not a ladder you're climbing or a game where you advance to the next level. It's more like a puzzle; you will see the picture no matter which piece you lay down first.

UNDERSTAND YOUR DIETARY RESTRICTIONS

Before we can start with the first pillar of acceptance, you need to know exactly what it is that you are accepting.

Let's start with the name. I have decided not to call it a disease. Celiac disease sounds too dramatic, in my humble opinion. It has the ring of chronic illness, which has no positive psychological impact on me. At the risk of sounding like my elementary school teacher, I have found the following to be true: words are powerful- use them wisely.

Initially, the information I was consuming on this topic led me to believe I was chronically ill. That I had a disease that won't go away until the day I die. I felt doomed and saw no way to ever be as happy as I had been again. That's one way to look at it.

I consciously see it differently now. I have called it a gluten allergy[1] instead. I'm allergic to gluten. That's it. Some people are allergic to cat hair, I am to gluten. Why am I the one with a disease, and they only have an allergy?

This is not me being oblivious to my condition. But for one, it makes it easier for others to understand since the term "allergy" is more commonly known. And in my experience, the word "allergy" is taken more seriously than "sensitivity" or "intolerance". Consequently, this increases the chances that the correct, necessary precautions are taken by others when preparing a meal for me.

More importantly, it has given me a more positive outlook on life. I need a positive perspective for my mental health. You might need one, too.

I invite you to ask yourself: How much negative impact do you feel when thinking of yourself as having "celiac disease?" Does it weigh you down? What for? Ask yourself: How do you want to think of this? How much weight, focus and attention do you want to give to that part of your life? You are the narrator in your own story. How are you going to tell it? It's up to you to decide. It will have an impact.

If you would rather call it "celiac disease," that's okay, too. Everyone's different. Maybe the seriousness of it all helps you to take the needed action and accept the new responsibilities that come with it. In my case, though, packaging the message in lighter wording helped me enormously.

---

[1] Compared to "gluten allergy", the terms "gluten sensitivity" and "gluten intolerance" are more commonly used. Due to personal experiences, though, I have decided to use the term gluten *allergy*.

I mentioned that I'm not being oblivious. I advise you to be as informed about celiac disease or your specific condition as you can/want to be. Once you have the facts down, you can deal with its real impact on your life. Don't be afraid to look the truth in the eyes. The sooner you look, the better. I often tell myself, "the truth is there, whether I look at it or not." Might as well get a realistic glimpse of what you're dealing with.

The focus of this book is not giving you recipes or advising you on the medical details of celiac disease. There are multiple great sources, and I see no benefit in duplicating what they say. However, I want to give you some pointers if you are new to the topic and don't know where to start. If you are already informed, feel free to skip this section.

∗∗∗

Here are the facts I needed to learn to live a healthy life without gluten.

Don't eat gluten (not even a crumb)

- ♥ Which foods contain gluten? In the beginning, I had a cheat sheet with me, so I could look it up if I wasn't sure.
- ♥ Grains that contain gluten include wheat, barley, rye, triticale, farina, spelt, kamut, wheat berries, farro, couscous, and sometimes oats (see below for further details).
- ♥ Let's look at the example of wheat. Wheat is in most noodles, bread, baked goods, certain condiments

(such as soy sauce), beer, etc. If you look at the ingredients label and you see "wheat," you know to avoid that product.

Watch out for contamination

- ♥ Do you know the game "the floor is lava?" If you touch the floor, you lose because you have touched the "lava." It's similar to contamination. If something has touched gluten, it's "lava," and you should stay away.
- ♥ In kitchens where foods containing gluten are made, there is a higher risk of contamination. You need everything to be super clean before you cook gluten-free. And remember that crumbs can fall into your food, so be aware. If you can, create a gluten-free zone in your kitchen.
- ♥ You will need appliances used only for gluten-free foods. I'm talking a toaster, mixer, wooden spoons or plates, anything with cracks that are hard to clean, and a waffle maker.

Watch out for social contamination (as I like to call it)

- ♥ A knife that's been on a gluten-bread should not be used for gluten-free foods. You can't share the same butter or pizza cutter when they're being used for gluten-free and gluten-containing foods.
- ♥ If your partner eats gluten and then kisses you- guess what? Some of that gluten may have gotten through.

Practical advice

- ♥ With those few facts, I think you can imagine how difficult eating out can be. So, talk to the waiter and/or the cook each time. Ask, ask, ask. There is no way around it.
- ♥ Read, read, read. I'm talking about labels. Each time you buy food, check the ingredients. Check frequently. You may think a certain product is gluten-free, but then they change the recipe, and it's not. Don't get too comfortable in this respect. Also, I've seen packages that had "gluten-free" and "can contain traces of gluten" written on the same box. Read everything to be on the safe side, especially the "ingredients" part.
- ♥ "Can contain traces of gluten" on labels is a tricky topic. From what I gather, it's a low risk. And if companies don't write it on the label, those foods may also contain traces of gluten. It's the same risk whether they put the sentence "can contain traces of gluten" on the package or not. You'll only ever be safe if you buy unprocessed food or "gluten-free" labeled food. Whether or not you want to take that risk is up to you.

Can be tricky: lentils, oats and flour

- ♥ Lentils: always check if there is wheat in them before cooking them. There is a risk of contamination because of how they are grown and harvested. If you find wheat in them, throw the wheat away. Wash the lentils (rinse them with water) and cook them. You can still eat the lentils. But for eating lentils from other cooks, beware. I usually decide not to risk it.

- ♥ Oats: oats are gluten-free, but the way they are grown (near wheat fields, for example) or processed exposes them to contamination. You need to buy gluten-free oats. Also, some bodies interpret oats as gluten. Test if you react negatively to oats or if they are no problem for you.
- ♥ Flour: even if it's flour made from something gluten-free, such as corn or buckwheat, if it doesn't say gluten-free on the package, don't risk it. The machines used to ground flour are a big risk of contamination. My mom didn't know this and made me a cake with that flour. I threw up for two days straight. If there are chips and a small part of the ingredients is "corn flour," and the rest is gluten-free, I suppose it's up to you to decide. It's been okay for me (but I'm aware this is a risk I take each time, and I rarely do it).

***

Those are just high-level rules to get you started. If you need more information on a certain topic, I recommend talking to a qualified doctor or nutritionist, finding good books or (carefully) looking online. Always find multiple sources and compare what they say. You will come across many opinions, and it's up to you to decide how much risk you want to take and what you're comfortable with.

There are so many good sources online, it's worth checking them out. Just google "celiac" or "coeliac," and you'll find many interesting articles on the topic.

Usually, each country has its own celiac foundation or something of the sort. Here are examples of official foundations in some English-speaking countries (ordered alphabetically):

Australia: https://www.coeliac.org.au/s/
Canada: https://www.celiac.ca/
New Zeeland: https://coeliac.org.nz/
UK: https://www.coeliac.org.uk
USA: https://celiac.org/

Become an expert on the topic. What can you eat, and what can't you eat? Which situations should you look out for? It can be overwhelming at first, but you can do this. You got this.

Once you've collected all the necessary facts, you have to put everything into practice. If you haven't gotten emotional up to this point, you probably will now. And if you do, don't worry, I have you covered. I've been through it, too.

When I first had to learn what it meant to live a gluten-free lifestyle, I was overwhelmed and deeply sad. I had done diets before, and it was tough, but it was never final. This is a "diet" I need to be on forever. A lifelong sacrifice. And for me, it came out of the blue. I couldn't even enjoy my favorite pizza one last time. It was a loss for me; I had to mourn.

Since food had been a huge source of comfort for me throughout my life, I struggled. What had once been my biggest source of joy was now a source of pain. This is very black-

and-white thinking, and we'll get to that later, but it's how I felt.

This new lifestyle was affecting me deeply, and I didn't know how to deal with it properly. I now know how to deal with it better, and I wish I had known back then. I am writing this book to help those in need at difficult times like these. So, let's dive right in.

Pillar 1: Acceptance

PILLAR 1: ACCEPTANCE

With change, there are several emotional reactions people normally have. The Kubler-Ross Change Curve is popular and often used to describe our reactions to change. It states you may go through five phases (to which I've added personal examples referring to my gluten allergy diagnosis):
1. Denial
   e.g., "There's been a mistake with the test. I don't have a food allergy."
2. Anger
   e.g., "Why me? This is so stupid! I hate this! I want to hit something!"
3. Bargaining
   e.g., "Maybe I can eat only a little gluten or make an exception on my birthdays."

4. Depression
   e.g., "I will never feel joy again, this allergy is sucking the fun out of my life. It's hopeless. I can't do this."
5. Acceptance
   e.g., "It's not great, but it is what it is. I can't change that. So, I'll have to learn to live with it."

You may skip a phase, but usually, you will be in most of these phases at some point. If the topic interests you, you will find many articles and books. I want to focus on the following: it ends with acceptance.

> I invite you to reflect. Which phase do you think you're in now? Which phases have you already been in?

Once you've accepted the situation, you can live your life again. You have accepted the new facts and can focus on finding the solutions that fit you. We're striving for active acceptance, where you not only accept but also actively try to make the best of the situation and act accordingly. See it as a sixth bonus phase, if you will.

Think of it this way: you are gifted with a house. Acceptance, sometimes called passive acceptance, would keep it exactly the way it is. With active acceptance, you keep it and make the best of it, decorate it, and make it your own. Granted, you didn't build a new house, and the house you got may not be 100% what you would have built or chosen. But this is the house you have, and you will make it awesome and wonderful. Now reread that paragraph and replace the word "house" with "life." That, my friend, is what we aim for in this book. That is active acceptance.

But how do you get there? Not everyone goes through all five phases. Some skip a phase. And how much use is it to force yourself to be depressed, hoping you can get to acceptance quicker? Probably not much.

Why should this interest you? It's important to be aware. Remember it and if you find yourself in one of those phases, know that you are reacting as many would and that such a life change can bring these feelings with it. Before accepting and then actively accepting, you may need to feel your emotions and process them.

FEELINGS AND WHAT TO DO ABOUT THEM

There are many ways to react to and feel about this situation. You could be grateful for the diagnosis. You now know what your body needs. At the same time, something was taken away from you. Your ability to eat gluten or whatever food you are allergic to. You probably want to be allergy-free. So, like a little child that has just lost their toy, our internal child throws a tantrum. If we are not aware, we react on autopilot. If you feel nothing and say you're fine, you might still be in denial.

In my case, my feelings were all over the place. I was frustrated that things had to change when they were better before. On Instagram, I often read quotes such as "make today so great that yesterday gets jealous" or "make each day better than the last." These "motivating" quotes imply life is an upward spiral. You are born, and from there, you thrive. You work hard, and life keeps improving. So how am I supposed to feel now when today is jealous of yesterday, not the other way around? Could I get a helpful quote on that, please?

Also, I kept reading posts and hearing stories of how every struggle makes you stronger. How every challenge is a blessing in disguise. How many people have gone through terrible things and come out "better than ever" on the other side? How people are grateful something "bad" happened to them because they now appreciate life more. Meanwhile, I'm lying under my desk in a fetal position crying my eyes out because this challenge isn't making me stronger. It feels like it's breaking me. So now what?

Closely linked to that was a feeling of guilt. Wars are going on in the world. People are starving. Some are losing loved ones. Others have a terminal illness. There are car accidents. There's human trafficking, and I'm depressed because I can't eat my favorite pizza?

This guilt is not constructive to your feelings at this stage. You need to validate your feelings and acknowledge them. If this is painful, you must mourn and process this. All the facts you used against yourself to feel guilty are true. We will need those later to gain perspective and find a way toward gratitude.

But for now, if you feel like it, you can and should cry because you can't eat your favorite pizza. You can even get mad; anger and depression are a part of this process. It's ok, cry it out. Feel your feelings for now.

Talk to people, talk to yourself, talk to a pet, journal, draw, do push-ups when you're mad, scream into water, sprint or jog while cursing, dance, throw yourself a pity party (not open end!), and find ways to feel your feelings and process them. A lot will come up, and the sooner you feel what you need to feel, the better.

> **Invitation to your pity party**
>
> I cordially invite you to join your pity party.
>
> When? This Thursday, 5 p.m.- 6 p.m., followed by a joyful, fun event of your choice.
>
> Please bring: a way to feel and explore feelings that works for you. If you'd like, bring a friend as well.

Always be patient and self-compassionate. You have every right to feel what you are feeling. Don't beat yourself up for not being "positive" enough or any other ideal way you want to react.

Later, I will give you advice on how to get a more powerful mind. To help briefly, though, here are sentences to tell yourself in those situations:

- ♥ It's normal that you're feeling this way. Your whole life has been turned upside down. Who wouldn't?
- ♥ I get it. Many would react as you are right now.
- ♥ Did you just beat yourself up when you were already down? No, queen/king/whatever you want to nickname yourself, we're not doing that. Not today.

♥ Yes, worse things are happening in the world. But this is still a challenging thing to deal with. You don't need to make yourself feel bad because it could be worse. There must also be room to process how this affects you, regardless of how it compares to anything else.

Now it's your turn. What are ways you like to process your emotions? If you are not sure, what are some things you'd like to try? Feel free to write them down here.

Activities that help me feel/process my feelings:

♥ _____
♥ _____
♥ _____
♥ _____
♥ _____
♥ _____
♥ _____
♥ _____
♥ _____
♥ _____
♥ _____

TRUE GAMECHANGER: EXPECTATION MANAGEMENT

My first attempts to make my life joyful included trying to act like everything was normal. I told myself that I didn't want this to define me. It was not supposed to be my identity. I did not want this to consume my life or influence my decisions. I was strong and will continue to live as I always have.

It was my attempt at being positive and resilient (looking back, it may have also been the denial or bargaining phase). So, I tried going on as best as I could, but it wasn't working. Life has just changed. Things have changed and will never be the same. That was the first form of acceptance, and it did not happen overnight. Once I was there, at the acceptance stage, a question grew louder each day: "So how am I going to deal with this?"

Remember how I said I would tell it like it is? How we need to look truth in the eyes? I took a while to get there. I wanted to get there earlier, but I didn't know how. The key for me was to accept certain truths that came with this new situation. This was a major turning point on my journey to active acceptance. I cannot stress it enough: this is crucial to joyfully living life with a food allergy and finding peace within. It transformed me and my attitude toward my new life for the better.

These truths gave me something I could process. I had feelings about each truth and needed to work through them. I needed to find solutions to each of them. Once I had done so, I found these truths are less surprising and ultimately have less power over you when they occur. It's a form of expectation management that comforted me in certain situations.

So, to make this easier, I am listing things you will also most likely have to accept. They are personal to me and my character. Adjust them to your situation. You may have something to add and find things that are not as relevant to you as they are to me. Nevertheless, I'm certain that you will find many very relatable truths that speak to you. Just know that you are not alone, and many with a diet restriction are going through similar situations to what you are going through.

Here are my truths, an explanation and my realistic mindset to them. I will also include my advice and thoughts here and there. You can see active acceptance shining through already. At the end of this chapter, you will find an overview of my truths without explanations.

Realistic Mindset- My Truths

This sucks. If I had the choice, I'd rather not have this allergy. (But I do, and I can't change that).

I searched high and low, but I found nothing so great about my situation that I'd choose having a gluten allergy over not having one. This may sound contradictory to my claim to live a joyful life with your food allergy. Ironically, this was a major step forward for me.

I have heard many arguments, but none were convincing. Eating healthier, for example. I can eat healthier without an allergy, thank you very much. Or how about building character and resilience due to a crisis? I've had and will have other crises, and if you ask me, the rate at which I'm building my character is going just fine, thanks.

What about a new appreciation for life? Okay, this one is the most convincing. But still, it did not console me since I'd rather come to appreciate life without going through this forced gluten-free scenario.

To sum it up, here is the bad news: this sucks. That's the reality. The good news is: you can still live a wonderful life. Life sucks sometimes. No worries, you can get through this and are stronger than you think. Besides, someone once told me: if the world didn't suck a little, we'd all fall off it.

It could've been worse. When it comes to limitations in life, I got lucky.

You would not believe some things others are going through. I invite you to check your privilege. More on that later when I address comparisons.

I have a new definition of luxury.

Luxury has become much more down to earth. For example, being at a gluten-free restaurant and eating everything without worrying about contamination. Finding a new recipe that tastes like an old favorite recipe. Winning a box of gluten-free products. It's a bittersweet truth, but to quote the internet, "it do be like that sometimes," you know?

But I've noticed how that positively affects the rest of my life. Having good people in your life is a luxury. Seeing a wonderful sunset. Eating my first strawberry in spring. Seeing it snow. Living in peace. Making time to do yoga in the morning or go for a walk. Discovering your favorite series is producing more episodes. These are all little things, but they are a luxury. They are not a part of everyone's life, and it's something to be so, so grateful for.

It was painful, but my food allergy has taught me you should not take anything or anyone for granted. Good things are a gift, not a right. And now I remind myself to say thank you for all I have, not eff you for all I don't.

I will be exposed to a new type of pain in my life. But also to a new appreciation for the good things in life.

Over the years, I have learned to appreciate the small moments in life. I still love food, even though my relationship with it has changed. Enjoying a delicious gluten-free meal (with people I love) feels precious. Friends and family have less time than they did when I was younger, so quality time with them is even more precious now. And sitting there with them, having gone through all these ups and downs, knowing that some things are still the same, is a comforting feeling. One I greatly appreciate.

I will have negative moments because of this. But there will also be plenty of beautiful ones.
This one sums it all up. It's my overall mantra.

Life is more than food. It does not always have to revolve around food.
This ties in with the luxury part above. Life has so much more to offer than food. I used to be so focused on food. Now, having been forced to seek happiness elsewhere as well, I know there are many sources of joy. I encourage you to find them for yourself.

***

New Lifestyle- My Truths
Meal-prepping is my thing now.
On some days, it would be nice to eat at the office cafeteria like my other colleagues. Being forced to meal prep all the time can be exhausting.

But I also try to see the advantages. I love being in control of what I eat and how much. Usually, it's healthier than what is offered in the cafeteria. It also saves money. Just call me the Meal Prep Queen.

Planning and making my food will take up some time.

It's a fact. If you need to plan nearly every meal (because you're either cooking or going out), it's just more time-consuming. But that doesn't mean you can't enjoy it, right? Maybe cooking and baking are new hobbies of yours? Maybe you can learn to love it? It's a way of taking care of yourself. It's become a ritual that shows me that I love myself.

Other advantages of making your own food include: being in complete control of which ingredients are in your meal (where my control freaks at? Can I get a "heeeey?" Say "hoooo!") and getting to bring the right amount for you. I can't tell you how often I was served super tiny portions and hungry after- or had too much on my plate and ate more than I wanted to. Making your food puts you in the driver's seat.

Despite all that positivity, I'll admit it can be exhausting and stressful to plan and make all my meals. I'm slowly realizing that I don't want it to be another stress factor and that I must consciously set aside time so this does not become unmanageable. I try to cook larger amounts that produce leftovers for another day. Then I thank my past self for cooking for me. Sometimes I ask others for help.

Do you know that saying, "You have 24 hours in the day, just like Bill Gates/Oprah/someone famous or successful?" While originally intended to motivate people, that saying is not fair to those with challenges that take up time. If you are forced to meal prep and cook a lot, you may have less time for other things. It's logical. Don't use this as an excuse not to go after your dreams, but also, don't beat yourself up if you find yourself under more time pressure than previously.

Life will feel more difficult at times.
Need I say more?

Gluten-free is often more expensive.
You can eat vegetables and rice, saving a lot of money. Generally, it doesn't *need* to be expensive to eat gluten-free. But chances are, if you want gluten-free meals or products like noodles, bread, or flour, you may have to pay more. I love noodles, but I don't need to eat them daily. Find a balance that works for you and your budget. If you can, treat yourself now and then. Life is meant to be enjoyed!

***

Interaction with Others- My Truths
I can't always be as spontaneous and flexible as allergy-free people.
You can't have it all. I was with a group of colleagues who had decided the day before where we would get lunch. I knew that place had nothing gluten-free, so I took lunch with me. Then, when we met for lunch, they spontaneously decided to go somewhere else. I would have been so stressed if I had been relying on the first restaurant. Does the new place offer gluten-free food? What if I need to order gluten-free food there a day in advance? Chances are, I would not have had anything to eat. I may have had to eat at the first restaurant alone or I would have pitched staying with the original plan to my team.

Most allergy-free people are used to walking past a restaurant, seeing it, thinking, "this looks good," and going inside. They probably don't know what gluten is anyway and assume you'll find something to eat- if they're even thinking about you. This is not malice. It's just what happens. Don't take it personally.

Don't feel bad for not being the cool, spontaneous friend for eating out. You can be spontaneous and flexible in other ways if that's important to you or if that's who you are. And if you're not, I'm sure you have many other lovely qualities your friends appreciate you for. Don't sweat it. The more they hang out with you, the more they'll know what's possible and what isn't. True friends will not use this against you. True friends want you to feel comfortable as well.

People will stare at my food and ask me what I'm eating.

Growing up, I've been the new kid several times, and my mission was always clear: blend in. Don't stand out. I suppose I still have this behavior anchored in me. I'd rather be left alone and do my own thing without questions.

When I bring a self-made quinoa pumpkin curry to lunch, or even if it's something obvious like pizza, there is usually always one person that stares at my food and comments on it. Even if it's nice, like, "Hey, that looks yummy," it made me uncomfortable because I failed at blending in. Of course, this is very personal, and I know not everyone will relate.

Check in on yourself when something makes you uncomfortable: why is this an issue for me? In my case: why should I blend in? What's wrong with people asking me what I'm eating? It's a nice conversation starter. If it annoys you every time, though, talk to people you often eat lunch with and tell them, "I know you probably only mean it in the best way, but I'm very self-conscious about always having to bring my food. I'd rather not talk about what I'm eating if that's ok."

This was just something that triggered me. Perhaps you have other triggers or other allergy-related situations that make you uncomfortable. Whatever it is, learn to accept it or change it. That way, you won't be surprised by it every time it comes up.

By the way, this still annoys me ever so slightly. I just can't shake the feeling. I'd just rather not talk about my food. I guess it's a preference. One colleague comments on my food every time and says it looks so yummy. Maybe it's the exposure, but I developed a different feeling toward it as time progressed.

On good days, where I can tap into the kindness of my heart, I see this for what it most probably is: a person without mean intentions, most likely trying to make me feel good about having to bring my own food. She means well and perhaps is empathetic and might feel bad for me. It's her way of sending love in my direction. That's how I like to see it. And with that mindset, I feel and react much more positively.

In certain situations, I will draw more attention to myself than I want to.

This one ties in with the previous truth. Sometimes, you need to tell people you can't eat the birthday cake they brought because you're allergic. You'd rather be polite and eat it, but you can't. You will stand out due to reasons you'd rather not stand out for.

I'm not always in the mood for standing out. Some days, I have low energy and want to blend in with the crowd. On those days, I remind myself of this truth.

I will have to talk to strangers a lot.
I have days when I want to fly below the radar and just not interact with strangers. For me, those are my introverted days, when I need to recharge alone. Then you're at the restaurant and need to talk about your gluten allergy and evaluate whether you feel it's safe to eat here. Ugh. So. Much. Hard. Work.

Some days you're just not in the mood. And that's ok. You can skip going out altogether or find an ally to ask for you. My partner helps me out sometimes on days when I'm super exhausted/have my introverted days.

If all else fails, it has helped me to know that I can talk to strangers even when I don't feel like it. When you're in the feels, you often forget. But you are not your feelings, you are your actions. And sometimes, even when I'm exhausted, I choose to be uncomfortable and do it anyway. It reminds me how strong I am. Kind of like the "do it scared" mantra, where you choose not to let your fear define you.

Still, my gluten allergy has made eating more difficult on my introverted days. Accepting that as a new truth has helped me better identify and manage those situations.

Not everyone will understand it. And maybe I don't need them to.
In my experience, those who don't have it, don't understand it (unless they are educated on the subject somehow or

they are empathetic people taking the time to understand). However, I'm done being upset with this one. A short person won't know how it feels to be a tall person and vice versa. You want to feel understood, but perhaps it's enough if you find a handful of great people you are close to who (attempt to) understand.

What matters is that you understand yourself. That you validate your pain. You have a right to be upset and you should be proud of how you are handling this. You don't need others to understand you to know that what you're going through is not a walk in the park. You don't need to prove yourself to anyone. You don't need their stamp of approval.

I will get reactions from people that will hurt me. And reactions that will uplift me.

Being a sensitive, empathetic person, this one hurt me the most. People are so unpredictable and if I'm having a bad day and someone says something inconsiderate, it will get to me. Especially at the beginning, when I struggled with my newfound allergy, I was so sensitive to the topic, and it made me feel like an easy target.

For example, when a waiter/waitress reacted rudely to my request or rolled their eyes at me because I'm "making a fuss," I got very upset, sad, and angry. One time I got served a salad with normal toast in it. I was confused. After going to great lengths to explain that I needed the salad and the dressing to be gluten-free, this was not what I expected.

I politely asked if the toast was gluten-free, which it turns out it was not. So, I asked the waitress for a new salad. "Can't you just take the toast off the plate and be done with it?" was her reply. She was pissed at my demand. I explained it was impossible to do it that way, and she took the salad to the back. Did I trust the next salad she offered me that came quickly? No. But to be honest, I was so upset with the whole situation, I lost my appetite. It was my first rude encounter, and I didn't know what to do. With a food allergy, you will be more exposed to these situations. You are setting a boundary, and not everyone reacts well to that.

The goal here is to find a way you would like to respond. Do you want to make a big deal and talk to the manager or not? Are you having a good day and want to practice standing up for yourself? Or is today just not your day, and you're going to cut yourself some slack and fight dragons some other time? I have found that standing up for myself can feel scary at first, but eventually, I will feel much better than feeling like the victim. That's my approach. Find one that works for you.

Also, standing up for yourself doesn't mean you have to get angry and start a fight. You can be kind and demanding at the same time. Experiment a little and find a style that works for you. Start small and see where it goes. Don't fear a little confrontation. In that situation, I could have given the salad back, said I don't feel comfortable eating there anymore, and not have had to pay for the salad, for example.

About two years later, I had a similar situation. I ordered a gluten-free salad and was given one with croutons. Something did not sit right with me, so I asked. Turns out the croutons were not gluten-free. So the waitress took the salad back and brought a new one. I checked it carefully and found a crouton in it again. Seems like the cook had just removed the croutons and given me the same salad. Sorry, but that's not how allergies work.

    I talked to the waitress again. I had lost all trust and just wanted to leave. I left without eating or paying for a salad, a victory. I stood up for myself and didn't accidentally eat gluten. Also, I didn't pay for something I can't eat.

    One sentence that's always helped me get through difficult times caused by other people is Hanlon's Razor: "Never attribute to malice that which can be adequately explained by stupidity." If someone's actions/words can be explained equally as well through their stupidity as it could be explained through them being mean to you, chances are it's their stupidity. Often, people are being stupid, not mean. "Stupid," in this case, refers to a lack of knowledge. They are not trying to bully you; they don't know about gluten allergies. This is your chance to educate them and help the next gluten-allergic person they encounter.

    Hurtful things from a stranger are one thing, but from someone close to you... that hits differently. I had one friend with whom I'd been friends for over 10 years. The way this friend reacted and treated me regarding my gluten allergy was not how I expected to be treated by a true friend.

    I had several negative experiences (also many non-food related ones) with her and tried talking to her about it, but she reacted poorly. Over time, I realized she's not the right friend for me. She's not a bad person, but it wasn't a good fit. My allergy opened my eyes to that. I've found it to be true that in times of crisis we find out who our true friends are.

Why am I telling you this? I want you to know that this allergy will put your relationships to the test. It will give people more opportunities to react well or poorly. And it is up to you to decide which behaviors you will accept. If something hurts you, you talk about it to them, and they don't try to improve the situation, then you may want to reassess if what you have is a real friendship. I'm not saying you must kick all your friends to the curb. But it is an opportunity to see who your true friends are. This, at least, is my approach. Feel free to see it differently.

It is also up to you to decide what you want from a friendship. You may value other things in a friendship than I do, and that's okay. Something that is a "red flag" for me may be okay for you. I'm simply encouraging you to stand up for yourself and to choose your friends mindfully.

Now the good part. There will be reactions that lift you up. I was on Crete, a Greek island, and showing the waiter my paper. This paper explained my gluten allergy in Greek and English. The waiter was very friendly and seemed genuinely concerned about the food I ate. He talked to the cook, came back, and asked questions. He made an effort. After we ate our meal, we even talked about my allergy. That I got it all of a sudden, and I had been living gluten-free for two years. He was genuinely empathetic and so kind. Faith in humanity restored.

As for people I know, I have also experienced many wonderful things. People who tell you it's no problem, and offer gluten-free options as well. People who think of you and bring gluten-free food to work. People who make the whole meal gluten-free, so you don't feel left out. People who stand up for you when you feel too weak that day. People who let you pick the restaurant when you go out. People who go to the same restaurant with you every time they see you and don't complain. Those are my kind of people. And when you have those people in your circle, who cares about the rude ones anymore?

You will experience pain and people will hurt you, but you will also experience joy and good people. Which one will you focus on?

Not everyone will take care of you and respect your allergy.
When it comes down to it, you must be there for yourself and be able to demand respect or leave. You're good to go if you've got yourself in your corner. Sounds easy, right? It's not! To this day, I'm still working on this. Learn to build your trust in yourself by speaking up when something doesn't fit. Think of yourself as your own lawyer. Represent yourself. Don't wait for others to do it for you or respect your allergy. You can demand respect. If you don't get it and it's crucial in that situation, know that you are strong enough to leave and you have the right to do so.

***

Going out/Social Gatherings- My Truths
There will be times when I am unprepared and have to be hungry.

I hate being hungry. I am your typical hangry (=angry because I'm hungry) person. Combine this with my need to have two to three "real" meals a day, and you have a hangry catastrophe! I'm kidding. But knowing myself well has helped me.

I always try to have a snack with me. An apple, chocolate, or some salted nuts, for example. Still, sometimes, you are surprised and have no chance to eat anything. It's happened several times already. I could find nothing edible and gluten-free. I even had recurring nightmares about this type of scenario. As I said, I love food.

This situation triggered me, which is why I've included it as a truth. I used to think, "why can't I just eat something like a normal person?" Not fun. More on that when I discuss comparisons and language. For now, I'll leave you with this: know your triggers. When this situation comes up nowadays, I already know that when I'm hungry, I am overly dramatic. I try not to take myself too seriously during those times. Like a storm that needs to pass. Once I've eaten something, I usually feel much better. Decide afterward if you were just hangry (hungry and angry) or if there may be an underlying issue you want to investigate.

I will see certain foods and get sad that I can't eat them.

It all comes down to this: I can't have everything. More specifically, I can't eat everything. That's the hard truth. What I like to do in these situations, though, is: I listen to Drake's song "Can't Have Everything." Because, like Drake, I "want a lot, can't have everything." If that's not your genre or you don't appreciate that joke I'm sure you'll appreciate this next piece of advice instead.

I also like to write down the food I'm sad I can't eat. Then, at home, I work on cooking that food myself. Can I recreate the food I've missed? Food FOMO (fear of missing out) is probably something everyone with a food allergy can relate to.

Just give it time. It will get more bearable. Explore the food you can eat and find new favorites there.

At times, I will feel excluded or like I'm not part of the group.

This one is a bitter pill to swallow. As a society, we often gather and eat with a group of friends, family, or co-workers. Eating together is a social interaction. I felt excluded because it seemed like no one cared about me. One time, a restaurant for brunch was booked without my consultation, and I had to bring breakfast myself.

On that day, I woke up earlier to make pancakes, which I then packed up and ate cold at the restaurant while everyone was having fun (except me, so it seemed). Those moments suck. It feels like you have to choose between not going (and missing out) or going and having to smile your way through all the pain, anger, and frustration you might feel. And, you guessed it, the obligatory "oh, wow, what are you eating?" question came multiple times. PANCAKES! I'M EATING PANCAKES, KAREN!

Those things are common in the beginning. Everything is new, and your social circle acts like it's the "same procedure as every year." Only that it's not. And sometimes you find out the painful way that something isn't working. The situation I mentioned earlier doesn't work for me anymore. I'd rather eat my pancakes fresh at home or bring something like yogurt, which still tastes fresh one hour later. Yogurt or overnight cereal can also be prepared the night before, saving stress.

Over time, you will develop life hacks, and I've included some in the book to give you a head start. Patience is required.

But the truth remains- even with my stress-free yogurt, I can't participate in eating what they are all eating. That will come up, and that's a part of your life now.

If it bothers you a lot, try talking to the host or hosting your own parties where you feel safe and can join in. Real friends will respect your feelings and do their best to make you feel comfortable. You'd do the same for them, wouldn't you?

For having this specific allergy, I am a minority.

Most people you hang out with don't have a gluten allergy. You'll have to explain to many what it is and what you can eat. That's just the way it is. I could tell you how you're a unique, special snowflake, but sometimes we want to be like everyone else, don't we? Don't worry. Because you know what? Everyone is a minority in some way. Maybe they look different, dress differently, have a different disease, or have gone through certain things you haven't gone through. You honestly don't know about all the challenges everyone else faces or their background. Just keep that in the back of your mind the next time you curse your food allergy. It doesn't make it go away, but it will help you gain an understanding of others and yourself.

Gluten accidents may happen occasionally. I'm doing my best, but I can't control everything.

I must balance fear and risk-taking. A certain fear and skepticism are healthy and very much needed. But it also needs to balance taking risks and learning to trust others. Each person needs to decide how they want to handle their situation.

Some may feel comfortable and happy being super careful and only eat at strictly gluten-free-only restaurants. For others, their soul would die a little, and they need to take more risks to be happy. Maybe you start one way and, over time, do things differently. Wherever you're at right now is fine.

I've always been a careful person and needed to loosen up a little in this respect. If I don't feel comfortable, I won't eat the food. But when I decide to take a risk, I need to at least enjoy it. What's the use of worrying all the way through? Where's the fun in that? That's my current mindset. It may change, over time. And that's okay. It's a journey, and it's a process. I'm figuring it out along the way.

When you take risks, and things don't go as planned, know you did the best you could and learn from that experience. Forgive yourself for not knowing then what you know now. Next time, you'll probably be better equipped; therefore, your experience will grow over time, and the risk will decrease naturally. Keep calm, and don't beat yourself up for it. Accidents happen.

Traveling did not get easier.

This resulted in a major life lesson for me. I like to travel, but I felt limited instead of feeling young, wild, and free. I'm here to tell you that you will have to do more research if you go elsewhere. Yes, you must plan more. And yes, you may even prefer to stay in places with a kitchen so you can cook for yourself. But it's all manageable. For inspiration, you'll find there are many travel blogs online where people share their experiences traveling elsewhere with their food allergies.

A new environment may be an adventure, but make sure to bring snacks. If you're traveling to a country where they speak another language, bring a paper with you on which you have printed a text explaining your allergy in their language. It often helps to show these to the waiter or the cook before you decide where to eat. You can find those texts online; they are my number one travel must-have. In addition to snacks, obviously.

And if all else fails, I must eat rice and beans for two weeks. I will survive! And I will travel as much as I want to. It may not be as comfortable as it is for my friends, but watcha gonna do? I'll have to make the best of it, I guess.

Also, I may not be able to travel as spontaneously as I used to. It requires so much more planning, and it does influence the way I travel. It's not as easy as it used to be.

On a more philosophical note, isn't it interesting how we take so much for granted until it's taken away from us? I'm still young and healthy enough to travel. One day, I may be older and unable to travel. We never know how life will progress.

So instead of looking back, mourning the days I traveled to try new foods, I've decided to look forward. These are the days I can travel. Perhaps, sometime in the future, I won't be able to go on travels as easily anymore. I may look back to these days as the good old days.

Sometimes it's fun to travel and try new, gluten-free foods. But sometimes, it's a pain. It comes down to this: I can't food-travel as I used to now that I have a food allergy.

But I can try other new things. I can't compare pizzas, but I can compare sunsets. And I've never met a sunset I don't like. I'm grateful for what I have. I'm young, wild, and gluten-free.

***

Those are my most important truths. As you've probably noticed, they can be specific to my character.
    What about you? Which of those resonated with you? Do you have some new ones you'd like to add for yourself? If you'd like, you can create a list of your truths on the next page.

My truths regarding my gluten-free lifestyle:

♥ _____
♥ _____
♥ _____
♥ _____
♥ _____
♥ _____
♥ _____
♥ _____
♥ _____
♥ _____
♥ _____
♥ _____
♥ _____
♥ _____
♥ _____
♥ _____
♥ _____
♥ _____
♥ _____
♥ _____

MY TRUTHS (OVERVIEW)

In case you'd like to revisit my truths without the explanations, here's an overview of my truths:

Realistic Mindset
- ♥ This sucks. If I had the choice, I'd rather not have this allergy. (But I do, and I can't change that).
- ♥ It could've been worse. When it comes to limitations in life, I got lucky.
- ♥ I have a new definition of luxury.
- ♥ I will be exposed to a new type of pain in my life. But also to a new appreciation for the good things in life.
- ♥ I will have negative moments because of this. But there will also be plenty of beautiful ones.
- ♥ Life is more than food. It does not always have to revolve around food.

New Lifestyle
- ♥ Meal-prepping is my thing now.
- ♥ Planning and making my food will take up some time.
- ♥ Life will feel more difficult at times.
- ♥ Gluten-free is often more expensive.

Interaction with others
- ♥ I can't always be as spontaneous and flexible as allergy-free people.
- ♥ People will stare at my food and ask me what I'm eating.
- ♥ In certain situations, I will draw more attention to myself than I want to.
- ♥ I will have to talk to strangers a lot.
- ♥ Not everyone will understand it. And maybe I don't need them to.
- ♥ I will get reactions from people that will hurt me. And reactions that will uplift me.
- ♥ Not everyone will take care of you and respect your allergy.

Going out/Social Gatherings
- ♥ There will be times when I am unprepared and have to be hungry.
- ♥ I will see certain foods and get sad that I can't eat them.
- ♥ At times, I will feel excluded or like I'm not part of the group.
- ♥ For having this specific allergy, I am a minority.

- ♥ Gluten accidents may happen occasionally. I'm doing my best, but I can't control everything.
- ♥ Traveling did not get easier.

***

It can be helpful for you to carry a list of these/your truths with you. Or to hang them somewhere. That way, you can see them (hopefully not be depressed by them) and remember them more easily. As a result, you will be even less caught off guard when those moments arise.

PAIN POINTS, UNDERLYING NEEDS, AND SOLUTIONS

The truths I mentioned also reveal some of my pain points: missing food, having a more complex (food-)lifestyle, wanting to be part of the group by eating the same food, others' hurtful reactions, feeling like a minority, having less flexibility, and less time.

You may find it helpful to identify your pain points. Once you have your pain points, you can work on finding solutions and reactions to them that suit you.

How do you identify your pain points? One way to do that is to simply brainstorm. What do you dislike about the current situation? What do you want to change? Where do you react emotionally? Write everything down. Do this for a few weeks and keep collecting. Things will come up in your everyday life that you can add to the list.

Another approach is to skip the brainstorming session and note things down when they come up. If you throw yourself a pity party, that can also be a great source of pain points to note down. We often vent to our friends, family, or partners. If they are willing to help, ask them to look over your list and see if you've missed anything. Or perhaps when you talk to them and complain or share things that bug you, take notes or have them take notes.

Once you have a list of pain points, look at them closely. You'll want to sort them into two categories: "can control" and "can't control." Or, as I like to call them: "change the situation" and "change my reaction." This is where the solution-driven mindset comes into play.

Let's look at two examples. First pain point: the kitchen is a mix of gluten and gluten-free products, which gives me anxiety. Second pain point: I miss having my chocolate chip cookie dough ice cream.

The first situation you can control. You can sort through things and have the top of the shelves be gluten-free territory, and the bottom gluten products. Or you can have a designated gluten-free corner where you feel safe. Perhaps other people in your household are also willing to eat more gluten-free meals with you. Maybe they do not understand the situation enough and you need to explain contamination to them. There are ways to "control" and change this situation so that you do not feel anxious when in the kitchen preparing food.

The second situation is not in your control. Unless you're the boss of an ice cream company, and perhaps not even then, most likely you will not be able to get them to make a gluten-free chocolate chip cookie dough ice cream. Side note: I already wrote a letter to an ice cream manufacturer and tried to motivate them to do so, but it didn't work... yet.

One approach is the "if you can't change it, accept it" mindset. I agree with that in some ways. Accept that, for now, they do not offer gluten-free chocolate chip cookie dough ice cream. But wait! We're not finished. There is something you can and should change, nonetheless.

Even when you can't control the *situation*, you can control your *reaction* to it. You need to shift problems from things that aren't in your control to things that are. So how can we react? You could work on your attitude towards the situation. You can change what is *within* your control.

You may not believe it, but I bought an ice cream machine. I also found an ice cream recipe book from the company that produced the chocolate chip cookie dough ice cream I was missing. AND I MADE MY OWN GLUTEN-FREE COOKIE DOUGH ICE CREAM! Sorry for screaming at you, but I'm still so excited about the whole thing.

It is more effort to make it, but I adjusted the recipe to be gluten-free. I used gluten-free oat flour for the cookie dough bites and it was so delicious! Not going to lie, if I did not have a gluten allergy, I probably would have bought it and saved myself the effort of making it. But this way, I reduced the sugar and added more cookie dough bites. And they are the best part, wouldn't you agree?

Making the best of each situation has become my motto. And this is a perfect example of that. You may not always be able to find the exact recipe. But you can try imitating the product you miss. That's one approach.

I want to encourage you not to give up. This will sometimes feel like an uphill struggle, but keep fighting for your happiness and solutions that work for you. Make the best of the situation you're in. That's all I'm asking.

If you can find no solutions right away, don't worry. Ask others for help and give it some time. I took nearly two years to come up with the chocolate chip cookie dough ice cream solution. And I needed to try several batches before I got the hang of it. But the joy I felt was indescribable once I had my own cookie dough ice cream.

Now, hold on. I hope I haven't lost you. If you're thinking, "she's crazy," "I can't cook," or "I thought you said you had practical advice," read on. Because I'm aware the answer to my celiac problems cannot always be to bake the world into a better place.

It's crucial to know that you may not always be able to solve everything. Not every recipe can be recreated. I got lucky with my ice cream example. In other instances, I was not so lucky. My mom made "honey bread" for us, a bread/cake made solely of whole wheat flour, honey, and eggs. I love that bread so much it hurts. And to this day, I could not recreate it successfully. Maybe I'll succeed one day, maybe I won't. But if I can't eat honey bread anymore, then I suppose that's the way things are now. I have learned to accept it or rather I have *reacted* with acceptance. I may cry about it once a year when I'm feeling low, but on most days, I'm all right.

***

Another interesting thing to do with your pain points is to reflect on which underlying needs aren't being met. For example, if I'm invited to a friend's birthday party and she has no gluten-free food for me, despite knowing my situation, I may feel hurt, angry, disappointed, or frustrated.

Which need causes me to feel these emotions? One may want to be part of a group or community and feel connected to those around me. Another may be not wanting to organize everything myself all the time. Being comfortable and not having to worry about what to eat. Feeling at ease and relaxed. Another need may be feeling valued. Having someone think of you and offer gluten-free options at their party.

You can brainstorm solutions even better depending on the need hidden behind those feelings. In the situation I described, you can focus on connecting with others through other means, not only food. You could talk to the host beforehand and have her organize gluten-free options (or bring some). Regarding feeling valued, you can reflect on ways this person has shown you they value you in other ways. Perhaps later, talk to this person about the situation.

In a nutshell, be honest with your pain points and why they are painful. Then, find healthy ways to alleviate the pain. Be it through taking action or being in control of your *reaction*.

In case this helps you, on the next page you'll find a template to help you jot down and work through some of your pain points. I've included an example to clarify how to fill it out.

	My example	Your situation
Pain point/ describe the situation	I can't buy the same cookie dough ice cream anymore	
Feeling(s)	Anger, frustration, sadness	
What are the underlying needs?	I want to treat myself while watching my favorite movies	
What's out of my control?	The ice cream manufacturer's decisions	
What's within my control? What are possible solutions?	Letting the manufacturer know of my dilemma, creating the ice cream myself, finding a different snack for myself	
Do I need help? From whom?	Need ice cream recipe	

***

Optional: make a list with me (yaaay!). On the next page, I invite you to list things that are/are not in your control. I've added some to get you started. You're welcome.

What's out of my control:
- Weather
- Karen's current questions about my food
- That it gets so dark during winter
- _____
- _____
- _____
- _____
- _____
- _____
- _____
- _____
- _____
- _____
- _____
- _____
- _____
- _____
- _____
- _____
- _____

What's within my control:
- ♥ Reaction to the weather
- ♥ My reply to Karen
- ♥ Making it cozy when it's dark out (lights, candles etc.)

♥ _____
♥ _____
♥ _____
♥ _____
♥ _____
♥ _____
♥ _____
♥ _____
♥ _____
♥ _____
♥ _____
♥ _____
♥ _____
♥ _____
♥ _____

LIFE HACKS FOR YOUR GLUTEN-FREE LIFESTYLE

Life hacks make everything so much easier. They are a big aid in helping you get more comfortable with your new lifestyle. Your life will be more convenient that way, and the "this is too hard" feelings will decrease.

Developing your new life hacks takes time and effort. So, I've written down some of my favorites to save you some time.

At home
My home is my sanctuary.

Make your home gluten-free if you can. I am lucky that my partner eats completely gluten-free with me at home. He has his beer and cereal, but other than that, I don't have to worry. I know I am such a lucky person to have this much support. Not everyone has this.

For those with more people living under one roof, find other ways you can feel safe at home. Maybe you need your own corner or shelf? Maybe you have your own pans, or your kitchen utensils are a different color/have a certain sticker on them?

Try to find ways to make sure you feel safe and comfortable at home.

Use sealing wrap to manage gluten-free dough.

When you first make gluten-free pizza, you will most likely notice that gluten-free dough is super sticky. It reminds me of the black stuff stuck to Spiderman in that third Spiderman movie with Tobey Maguire. But I digress.

There are ways to tame this sticky monster. You will need to place the dough on parchment paper and then place the sealing wrap on top of the dough. Kind of like a sandwich. You have the paper and the sealing wrap on the sides and the dough in the middle. Then use a rolling pin on top of the sealing wrap to flatten the dough. A nice side effect is that the rolling pin doesn't get dough on it, so you need not clean it.

A not-so-nice side effect is the waste it produces. But hands on my heart, I have tried but not found another way to deal with sticky gluten-free dough.

You can also use gluten-free flour on your hands so that you can touch the dough without it sticking to your hands. Whether or not this works depends on the dough you're working with. Feel free to experiment a little.

Buy gluten-free bread on sale/bake your own bread, and put it in the freezer.

Sometimes you'll find gluten-free bread on sale because it's about to expire. Pop that bread in the freezer, and voila. When you want some bread, take a slice out of the freezer and put it in the toaster.

When I bake bread myself, I also like to freeze some of it (sliced). There's something about a toasted bread slice that's just so yummy every now and then. And I'm not always in the mood for baking my own bread ahead of time. This saves you a lot of time and is a nice meal-prep option I like.

Xantham Gum makes a difference.
This helps to reduce crumbly, falling-apart disasters when you bake. Add a tiny bit (about one teaspoon per one cup/120g of flour).

Have snacks ready to go.
Sometimes, I don't have time to go shopping before I visit friends or they visit me. Other times, I spontaneously need to go somewhere and don't have time to make a snack from scratch. I have found that in those moments, something packaged and gluten-free is a lifesaver.

***

Socializing
Bring something to eat.
Is someone celebrating their birthday? Bring a gluten-free cake as part of your gift. That way you don't need to stress about the cake they baked.

I also like bringing a bag of gluten-free chips and some soda/wine to parties. It's a nice gesture, and it assures me that I'll have at least something to eat/drink if all else fails.

Talk to your host/hostess beforehand.

That way, you know if they are serving anything gluten-free. I brought gluten-free bread myself once, and the rest of the buffet was gluten-free (I was careful about contamination). Small things like that can help the host/hostess and make you feel at ease.

Find time to try new restaurants in your area.

When you're tired and you don't want to cook or when you spontaneously have guests coming into town, that's not the time to find a new restaurant.

Instead, take some time on the weekends to try new restaurants that work for you. I am setting myself the goal of doing this once a month. I have a list where I collect my experiences and a map where I collect all the successful restaurants. That way, I forget nothing and always have great places to recommend.

Invite people over for dinner.

This is not for everyone. But it's nice to have people over and be in control of the food offered every now and then. Especially for birthday celebrations. Plus, it usually saves a few bucks (and nerves, depending on your restaurant experience).

***

On-the-go

Always have snacks with you.
Life's just better when you're not hungry, am I right?

Bring a spoon/fork with you.
Hear me out. Sometimes you must be creative, go to a tiny grocery store, and see what you can find. It helps to have a spoon or fork with you for those occasions. A spoon should do it in most cases. A fork or a knife can be a little sharp/threatening. Therefore, it may not be such a great thing to take everywhere you go.

To-go gluten-free supermarket options you can get almost anywhere:
- Fruit
  - Apples
  - Bananas
  - Berries
  - Cherries
- Baby carrots & a dip (e.g., hummus, guacamole, peanut butter)
- Cucumber is theoretically also possible, but I don't like not being able to wash it properly beforehand
- Yogurt (combine with fruit/honey/nuts/chocolate sprinkles)
- Nuts (natural or salted)
- Cheese (bonus points if you brought your own bread with you)
- Smoothies

- ♥ Juice
- ♥ Salad (sometimes gluten-free)
- ♥ Chocolate (sometimes gluten-free)
- ♥ Protein bars (sometimes gluten-free)
- ♥ Chips (sometimes gluten-free)

***

Traveling and Vacation
Do some research & contact the hotel beforehand.

Before booking a hotel, I usually contact them about gluten-free options. Or I go with a version where I don't buy breakfast at the hotel and plan accordingly.

It's also helpful to research the area where you're staying and see if they have any gluten-free restaurants. There's a lot that can be found online. I plan my days and see if there are any good restaurants nearby for places I want to visit. Getting a general feeling of how the country is set up in terms of gluten-free will also help you determine how much food to bring with you.

Try booking a room with a kitchen or at least a fridge.

You may need to buy food at a local grocery store to get by. Do yourself a favor and book a room that supports your food allergy needs.

BYOF: Bring your own food (especially on airplanes).

You know how you can order a gluten-free meal from some airlines? Yeah. That's great, but when the flight gets canceled, and they reschedule you to another one, guess whose order gets lost? Yes, yours. Or sometimes the meal "didn't make it on board." Whoops. Guess who's starving now? You are.

Not with me! Bring your own lunch/dinner/whatever, at least as a backup. Find something that works for you. I like making a quinoa salad with corn, kidney beans, or chickpeas. Something I can eat cold, and that won't go bad super quick. Don't make soup- chances are that's too much water, and they won't let you pass security with that.

Bring a can of tuna to pimp a salad.
I don't like tuna all that much. But I still thought this was brilliant and wanted to share it. It may inspire you to find similar life hacks.

So, the idea is to bring a can of tuna with you when you travel. Then, you can buy a normal salad somewhere (gluten-free) and add tuna to it. That way, you have protein, and you won't be hungry again 15 minutes after eating the salad.

If you don't eat it, no worries. It's not open. And if all else fails, you may have to eat the tuna with nothing.

Have backup food in your suitcase (oats, bread, noodles, flour).
Imagine this: they say they have gluten-free food, and you arrive and find out it's not enough. It's good to have some gluten-free oats for the hotel breakfast. I like to combine those with yogurt and fruits. Sometimes I use them to make cereal. It's just one essential item that can help you get creative with the breakfast buffet.

The same goes for bread/toast. But this one's more difficult because it takes up a lot of space in your suitcase. Also, once opened, it doesn't last as long. So, depending on how long you're traveling, this may not be ideal.

When I travel to a small island or small town, I also like to bring gluten-free noodles. Most grocery stores have many naturally gluten-free items you can cook with. They sometimes lack specific gluten-free items, though. That's why I like to bring some noodles with me. Otherwise, rice is also a good option to buy locally.

Another thing I like to do is to bring some (buckwheat) flour for a pancake recipe I love. The rest of the ingredients can usually be found locally. That way I can buy eggs, milk, and sugar at a normal grocery store and then still make gluten-free pancakes. It saves me the stress of looking for gluten-free flour. Having this flour with me has made my day many times.

Use toaster bags.

There are toaster bags for celiacs. You can put your toast in them and place the bag in the toaster. That way, you don't have to worry about contamination. When I travel, I like to do this. That way, you are prepared and can have toast for breakfast without having to worry.

If there's a buffet, try to be the first one there.

Buffet = contamination nightmare! I always like to arrive at buffets before the big crowds and load up my plate. That way, I don't have to worry about contamination as much.

Also, if possible, I try to be picky and take food from places in the bowl where it seems like no one's been yet. Not very scientific, but I get a gold star for trying, right?

With eggs, I usually go for hard-boiled eggs at a buffet. The contamination risk is lower, and I feel more at ease. And always ask questions- the scrambled egg is not always gluten-free.

Fruit such as apples or bananas is a great go-to at a breakfast buffet. Plus small yogurts that are individually packaged.

Bring a "letter to the cook" in the language of the country you're traveling to.

Do some research online and find a "letter to the cook" or a text describing your allergy (allergy translation) that you can give to someone cooking for you. I like to have it in English and the language they speak. Then, before sitting down at a restaurant, I show the waiter this letter and ask whether they can cook a meal for me. If they can, I sit down and enjoy. If not, I continue my search. This has worked well in the past.

Pillar 2:
Support Network

PILLAR 2: SUPPORT NETWORK

No (wo)man is an island. Life is easier with the right support network around you. Let's look closely at what kind of network you could benefit from. Reflect on how your network is set up as you read this section. Are you happy with it or would you like to make changes? Is there anything missing? Is there anything you want to try and see if it works for you?

I have found the following areas are most important to look at: yourself, friends and family, gluten-free community, and professionals. Let's look at each area more closely and then I'll give you some advice on dealing with non-supportive people. At the end of the "Pillar 2" part, I've got something special for you: life hacks on how to "clap back" when confronted with difficult conversations.

YOURSELF

It sounds so cliche, but it's true: you must be on your own team and stand up for yourself. You will need to get out of a victim mentality (if you ever were in one) and accept that you are responsible for yourself and your reaction in this situation.

You are not a victim. Yes, this is happening to you. And maybe it's not fair. It also doesn't matter whose fault it is. What matters is that you try to do the best you can with life as it is now. What can you do to make this situation better? How much more time and energy will you lose fighting what is? Why not use that time and energy to build a new, wonderful life?

You've seen many examples of accepting responsibility throughout the book. I hope they inspire you to be active when it comes to accepting this food allergy. You must take this mindset into your life and everyday scenarios. I know that you can do it. You have to start somewhere.

Another thing to remember. When you accept responsibility for yourself, it's like being your own parent. The aim is to be a good parent to yourself. If your child is sitting there crying, you would console it. See what's going on and try to help it. If your child felt uncomfortable or mistreated in a certain situation, you would stand up for him/her and say something. That's how you need to treat yourself.

Learning this takes a long time, and I wonder if you're ever done learning it. It's part of the wonderful journey called life; to actively work on this is a gift you give yourself. And eventually, this will be a gift you give the world because we all need to learn to be better parents to ourselves.

So, you need to count on yourself. Part of that is standing up for yourself. Because sometimes, if you don't, no one else will. Correct the situation if someone does not treat you as gluten-freely as they should.

Also, you need to make your mind your friend. It's not always as easy as it sounds. You will find more on this later in the book. Stay tuned.

***

Another thought here is that you are a part of a network or a community. Giving others advice or contributing to their well-being can also help you find a sense of purpose.

Maybe you want to open up a gluten-free restaurant or become a food blogger. It's a way of turning your pain into something productive, useful, or beautiful. A way of helping others in a similar situation. With my book, I am hoping to do just that.

FRIENDS AND FAMILY

This is the most difficult one. Usually, these should be the people who support you no matter what and you should be able to count on them. Sadly, this is not always the case. For more on that, I've created a part on "non-supportive people" which will follow later.

Let's say we don't run into those problems yet. You will need your friends and family to be informed on the topic. There are multiple ways to do this. You could host an info event at your place. Or you could talk to them separately. I've noticed that things get repetitive, and the questions are often the same. There's a difference between people who cook for you often and people you see now and then. Those that cook need more details.

That's why I created my pamphlet with the most important things my friends/family need to know. I explain what contamination is and which foods are good or not good. How important it is to read labels. And I've also created a decision chart that helps to determine if something is okay for me to eat. Just something helpful if someone wants to check.

I've also stressed that they can call me at any time and ask questions. I've cooked with them together as well. That way, they have a more hands-on approach to learning the art of gluten-free cooking.

Be clear this is an allergy that is not going anywhere. It's here to stay. And yes, a little gluten does hurt. And no, I'm not being picky. Give them some time to adjust and learn. They'll get the hang of it soon, like you.

Writing down which family members you need to inform can be helpful in the beginning. Here's a checklist to get the party started.

Informed family members:

♥ _____

♥ _____

♥ _____

Family members who still need to be informed:

☐ _____

☐ _____

☐ _____

How/when I want to inform them:

☐ _____

☐ _____

☐ _____

GLUTEN-FREE COMMUNITY

It's nice to have allies. Someone who also has an allergy- it doesn't even need to be the same one. There's a certain comfort in talking to others who understand what you're going through. No need to explain, they've felt the same thing at one point. I've found that, as I get older, there are more people with food intolerances. Is it the age? Is it the times we are living in? Who knows? But I know more people with diet restrictions are out there than you may think.

Having someone with the same allergy is a bonus. You can exchange advice and try restaurants together. It's a wonderful opportunity. You feel less like a giant among dwarves and more like a... well... a giant among giants. Contrary to common belief, it feels nice to be average sometimes.

Now, how do you meet those people? One thing is to be open about your food allergy. This may lead to others also opening up about theirs. Another way is to look online. For example, you will find celiac groups on Facebook. Following gluten-free bloggers on Instagram or in general, the internet also gives you a sense of community. Sometimes, there are organizations/clubs/gatherings in your area you can look for (or organize one yourself).

You will also meet many people with a similar diet when you go to specific gluten-free events. Just try things out and see what you find.

Also, have you ever googled "celebrities who don't eat gluten" or "celebrities who have celiac disease?" I don't want to drop any names, but seeing how others have a similar fate is interesting. I also looked for interviews where they talk about their food allergy. It's very comforting and inspiring.

You will see that my community advice is not solely based on actually meeting people. Being part of a Facebook group and reading the posts/comments can help you feel like part of a community. Or reading what bloggers have to say. You decide how active you want to be in your role as a community member. If you want to be one at all.

What I have found, however, is that it's very beneficial, especially initially, to be part of a community of people sitting in the same boat. Their advice can save you some time (and mistakes), and in terms of moral support, it's great to hear you're not in this alone. Your reactions are normal, and there's a certain sense of comfort in knowing that most people in your shoes feel the way you do.

I am part of a celiac group. We get together about every two months and spend some time together. Sometimes we eat something gluten-free, and sometimes try out a new activity. Meeting so many new people can be nerve-wracking, but if you have the chance, I'd say try it! I enjoy the stories we exchange and the reactions I get when I tell them about something that happened to me.

What groups do you want to be a part of? If they don't exist, would you be willing to create one? Perhaps this checklist will prove to be helpful.

Gluten-free communities I want to participate in:
- ☐ Facebook group
- ☐ Local group
- ☐ School club
- ☐ _____
- ☐ _____
- ☐ _____
- ☐ _____
- ☐ _____

PROFESSIONALS

Who are your doctors? Do they know about celiac disease, and can they answer your questions? Should you look for an additional "celiac expert doctor?" It is recommended to do yearly health checkups as a celiac to see if everything is fine (e.g., have you been eating gluten by accident and need to adapt your diet?). This is where a network can come in handy. They may give advice on which doctors you can visit.

Another area where professionals are needed is nutrition. In the beginning, I had a few sessions with a nutritionist who was an expert on celiac disease. She helped me understand what contamination was and how to avoid it. What I needed to watch out for. She gave me advice and tips on how to handle this new allergy. I highly recommend doing something similar if you're new to your allergy.

My partner was with me for those sessions, and I suggest you do the same for your sessions. Take someone with you- a friend, a partner, a family member. Just someone else who you can talk to about this afterward and who can help you transition to your new allergy-friendly life. It's also a huge bonus you have one person less to explain everything to. Plus, they might even help you explain it to everyone else.

When you're new to the topic, you rarely know what you're doing in the kitchen. Baking, especially, is difficult for a gluten-free newbie. To spare you some frustration, I suggest you take a course on how to cook/bake gluten-free. It can be online or in person, but it's just so much better when you have a person there with you who gives you advice and who you can ask if questions come up. Invite friends and let's go!

If doing a cooking course is not your thing, then I recommend searching for gluten-free recipes online. Be aware that not every recipe will be a success, which might not have anything to do with you. Some bloggers are better than others, so find one that fits you. I like to print out successful recipes and collect them in a binder. That way, I always have great recipes to return to when I'm not in the mood to try something new.

Building up a new repertoire of recipes will take some time. So be patient. I love pizza so much that they called me the "Pizza Queen." I'm serious. So obviously, a top priority for me was mastering a gluten-free pizza recipe. Once I had that down, I knew it would all be okay and had the strength and courage to try other recipes.

Also, if you're new to the whole thing or not that good at baking/cooking, I suggest trying meals naturally gluten-free first. They will be easier and less frustrating. Anything with gluten-free flour is an advanced recipe. So maybe don't try those if you're having a bad day.

My advice? Start with recipes using gluten-free noodles. Preferably ones made of corn or rice flour because those taste like the noodles you're probably used to.

Which recipes do you want to recreate? Can you find some online or do you need expert advice on them?

Food	Found recipe online?	Is expert help needed?
Cookie dough ice cream	Yes	No

DEALING WITH NON-SUPPORTIVE PEOPLE

Let me just say this: life is too short and precious to spend with people making your life hard. I've already listed examples of non-supportive friends, and I had to reexamine what friendship is for me. I had to stand up for myself.

I speak up when something bothers me in a kind, calm manner. I let the other person know how what they're doing is affecting me. And I hope for a kind, understanding response. I do not always get one, but those have been people who do not have my best interest at heart. These are not the people I want to keep in my life. And that's ok. I don't have a dramatic falling out, but when it doesn't fit, it doesn't fit.

However, this is *my* approach to the topic. I want you to find an approach that works for *you*. I like to be vulnerable and jump in when I see a problem. I like to talk about it no matter how awkward the conversation will be. Not everyone is that way, and not everyone needs to be. Some people don't mirror this approach, and I respect that. Still, if something bothers you and you don't speak up, you will probably become resentful or continue to suffer.

Friends are easier to talk to than family. Friends are chosen. Family isn't. For friends, you don't have to continue the friendship forever. With family, it's often more difficult to get some distance. You must judge for yourself how you would like to respond. For me, setting the right expectations made a big difference.

Some family members don't understand my allergy, no matter how often I explain it to them. My grandparents, for example, bless their hearts, just don't get it. I try to explain it, but it's just such a foreign concept to them. I feel like I'm speaking a different language. I know this is not bad intent on their end. I bring my own food when I visit them. I made a cake for them and stopped by recently. It was a very pleasant afternoon.

Next, a word on strangers or people you barely know. Don't give them too much power over your emotions. Don't let a "stupid" waiter or waitress ruin your day. It's just not worth it. With strangers, try to take the approach of not taking it personally. How could you? They don't know you. And you don't know them. You don't know what they've been through or are going through.

So, when they make you feel like a diva for telling them you have a gluten allergy, don't let it get you down. You know yourself well enough to know whether you're a diva. They are not the judges, and you are not on "The Voice" singing your heart out in the hopes that they will approve and push that red button to turn around.

They can call you whatever they want, it doesn't have to impact you. They don't get to say if you're acting like a diva. If they are not serving you the food you ordered, send it back and walk away. The world is a big place. Not everyone you meet will be kind to you, but that doesn't mean you are worth any less.

LIFE HACKS: CLAPPING BACK

Everyone who has dealt with food allergies can tell you so many sentences they have heard repeatedly. Reactions you get so often that life feels like a broken record player.
    Now and then, however, some reactions leave us speechless. Did they just say that? I can't believe it! Now you have the choice: how do you want to react? I like to react in a classy manner. One that doesn't attack the other person but creates a somewhat friendly atmosphere and opens the door to a conversation. A different response is more appropriate in some situations, but I generally try the peaceful approach first.
    But what does that look like in practice? Don't worry, I got you covered. Here are tactics and replies you can use in moments you do not feel prepared for (until now).
    First off, aim to be calm. You don't need to get defensive. Using humor can help. Practice makes perfect, but you're good to go if you're courageous. Be aware that often, these

people don't know what they are talking about. You're representing the "food allergy community," raising awareness and speaking on their behalf. What you say now will likely educate someone and could benefit your food allergy community.

Nevertheless, if it gets too rude, I have other strategies. Use them when needed.

What's also helpful is to have an elevator pitch ready to go. It's a statement that sums the situation up briefly. Imagine you're in an elevator and have only a few seconds to get your point across before the other person leaves.

Here's mine:

I have a serious gluten allergy. It's genetic, so I will always have it. If I eat gluten, I will have an allergic reaction, so I need to be careful not to do so. Even a small crumb can cause harm. Gluten is found in grains, including wheat, rye, spelt, and barley. Things I cannot eat usually include bread, pasta, crackers, cake, baked goods, several beverages like beer, and processed items. For me, it's not a lifestyle choice but a necessity, and so I want to say thanks in advance for respecting that and respecting me.

All right, now let's get to the strategies.

Strategy 1: The umbrella strategy (the right mindset)

When someone says something stupid, it may say more about them than it does about you. You can choose not to comment and let it go. If their comments are like rain, you have an umbrella in your mind you open and keep yourself dry.

To do so successfully takes some inner work. You can take what they are saying and turn it into a compliment. For example, if they say, "Still doing this gluten-free trend, huh?" you can tell yourself they admire your determination.

You could also decide their response reflects their own problems. If they say, "Don't tell the waiter you have a gluten allergy. That's so embarrassing!" it tells you they care a lot about what other people think of them.

Strategy 2: Educating them

Sometimes people don't know what you're dealing with. They say incorrect things. Here's a list of some sentences I've come across:

"I baked this great cake. I've added cinnamon, sugar, milk, eggs, and wheat flour. And I've included gluten-free flour! You should be able to eat it then."

"Oh, just a little bit won't do any harm!"

"Can't you make an exception?"

These sentences scream at me: I HAVE NO IDEA WHAT AN ALLERGY IS OR WHAT TO DO WHEN SOMEONE HAS ONE.

Here's your time to shine. Sum it up in a short sentence and help them with a metaphor. "Have you ever heard of the game 'the floor is lava'? Having an allergy is like that. Only for me, on the inside, gluten is lava. So anything that contains gluten, I have to avoid. You know?"

Here's another one (shout out to DJ Khaled #anotherone): "Contamination is a lot like salmonella. You don't see whether or not it's on the food, but it has its consequences, nonetheless. Eating that food will make you feel like crap the next few days."

You will also need to get more comfortable respectfully saying no and sticking to your boundaries. A colleague brought a cake to our office and said she made it gluten-free. Meanwhile, I had sweaty palms because I didn't know which mixer she used, and the risk of contamination was quite high.

I told her, "I'm so happy you thought of me and made the cake gluten-free! Thank you so much, I'm touched." Then we had some small talk. I asked, "Can I ask, did you use a normal mixer when you made it?"

She replied she had to which I said, "I was worried about that. There's no way you could have known, but mixers usually suck up some of the flour when you use them. So if you've used that mixer before with wheat flour, chances are the mixer spit out some of that wheat flour, and now some of it is in the cake. I'm aware this can seem paranoid or picky, and it's not easy for me to say this, but I'm just worried that the cake is contaminated."

She understood, and it was no problem. Now she knows, and maybe next time it will be different. What's important is that I stood up for myself.

One tip: the earlier you stand up for yourself, the better. If I had said nothing, she may have thought everything is fine and baked another cake. What then? Do I say something then, or is it weird because I said nothing to the first cake she made? Know that it's never too late to stand up for yourself, but also know that it's easiest if you do so from day one. So don't be hesitant.

Here's an idea I had afterward. In that situation, I could have also taken one piece home for my partner and then told her the next day how much he enjoyed the cake. That way everybody's happy!

Strategy 3: The definition strategy

This one will always work. Someone says something that sounds like an insult, and you take that insult, redefine it and make it sound like a compliment.

For example, to "You're being so picky," you could reply like this:

"If by being picky you mean that I'm taking care of my health, then yes, I'm picky."

It's simple, and it always gets the job done. Love it.

Strategy 4: Copy & paste sentences

They say something, and you use the same sentence structure and say what you feel. Try to do it politely is my advice.

For example, to "It's a shame you can't eat this bread. It tastes so good!," you could reply like this:

"It's a shame you don't know how to be empathetic. That's so annoying!"

Strategy 5: You say it best when you say nothing at all

If you have that Ronan Keating song stuck in your head now, you're welcome.

This strategy is great because you can use it in 100% of the comments made. You don't say anything. You stare at them, raise your eyebrows as if to say, "I can't believe you just said that," and lightly shake your head if you need to. Then you look away.

Or maybe you are less dramatic. Either way, you decide not to comment.

Strategy 6: Mh?

Pretend you didn't hear what they said. Ask them to repeat it. They probably will rephrase their sentence and take some of the heat out. It also gives you some time to think about your response.

Strategy 7: Empty replies

Some replies are like a dead end for conversations. They can always be used, and sometimes they don't even communicate much. Some of those include:
* You don't say.
* If you say so.
* Agree to disagree.
* Who knows?
* Oh, really?
* Yeah, yeah.

Strategy 8: Replying with a question

You can almost always use this one. You simply ask them a similarly stupid/awkward question back.

You risk offending the other person with this. Remember: tone is everything. If they say it in a joking way and you know they mean no harm, you can reply in a joking way. After your reply, you can both have a good laugh.

If someone's tone is rude, a rude tone with this strategy will also do the trick. Use with caution.

For example:

-So, you're also trying the new gluten-free trend I hear? Do you know that won't make you famous?

-Didn't you hear? Gluten-free is not a trend anymore. Do you know how to stay up to date?

Strategy 9: What do you mean? #justinbieber

Just ask them to elaborate. Chances are they will soften their first wordings, creating a better atmosphere for a pleasant conversation.

For example:

-Still have a "gluten allergy" I see?

-What do you mean?/What are you trying to say?/Excuse me?

Strategy 10: Agreeing (a little too much)

The aim here is to overdo it so obviously that everyone will know you're being sarcastic. It can come across as a little annoyed or rude, so feel the room before using it. You can also use it to take it to a new level if the other person isn't getting it and you feel a different approach is in order.

For example:

-Do you think not eating gluten will solve all your problems?

-Yes, as a matter of fact, I do. I also think I will get a Nobel Prize for my gluten-free lifestyle. And then later, Santa Claus might give me a genie to grant all my wishes.

Strategy 11: Time out

Use this strategy when the other person has gone too far. Show them they cannot talk to you in this way.

For example:

-What is this stupid gluten-free diet you're doing? Are you that desperate for attention?

-I will not be talked to in this manner. Either you rephrase that sentence, and we can discuss it in an orderly fashion, or I will have to end this conversation.

Strategy 12: Non-cooperative

Just because someone asks a question does not mean you must answer it. If someone starts a conversation, it does not mean you must play along.

For example:

-Explain again why you think this gluten-free diet is good for you?

-I don't have to explain anything to you/I don't owe you an explanation.

Or:

-You look tired, must be the gluten-free diet.

-I'm not interested in having this discussion with you. Let's change the subject.

Strategy 13: TTYL (Talk to you later)

Move the discussion to another date. Perhaps it will never take place.

For example:

-Tell me again, how is your gluten-free diet different from the other fashion diets you read about these days?

-Let's discuss this later.

Strategy 14: Asking for advice

If they're so smart, ask them what they would do.

For example:

-It's a bad idea to make gluten-free noodles now.

-What are you suggesting we cook instead?

Strategy 15: Deny, deny, deny

Simply disagree.

For example:

-That gluten-free diet will never work. You will always have stomach cramps.

-I disagree. You will see, I will get healthy again.

***

Other strategies exist, but I find those are the most useful ones. Trying to memorize them all will most likely leave you unable to react quickly when the time has come. Remember your favorite strategies, and you're good to go.

Pillar 3:
The Right Mindset

PILLAR 3: THE RIGHT MINDSET

This part on the third pillar discusses how to deal with your thoughts and how to make them work for you, not against you. It's about making your thoughts your (true) friend. Ultimately, it's about having an attitude toward life that benefits you and those around you.

I have found the following to be the most important elements to master and will discuss them in more detail:

- ♥ Take back your power (responsibility and control)
- ♥ Healthy optimism and being solution-driven
- ♥ Confidence and boundaries
- ♥ Perspective and gratitude
- ♥ Friendly thoughts
    - ♥ Watch your language
    - ♥ Comparisons
    - ♥ No rumination
- ♥ Humor
- ♥ Dealing with stress

TAKE BACK YOUR POWER

Have you heard the saying, "happiness is a choice?" When I have bad days, it's the last thing I want to hear. That doesn't make it any less true, though. I read an interesting book where journalist Maike van den Boom traveled to the 13 happiest countries in the world and interviewed people to find out why they were so happy. One finding was that many people, despite very difficult circumstances, consciously chose to be happy.

It can't be that easy, can it? I got little sleep last night, it's Monday, and it's raining. How am I supposed to choose to be happy?

I've tried it, and... it works. I'm sorry, but it does. Now and then, it seems we need to remind ourselves to be happy. It's a feeling we can feel anytime we want. Disclaimer: I'm talking about mostly normal circumstances. I don't want to offend anyone going through traumatizing times or those with a mental illness (but even then, I wonder if this could help).

Whether you want to admit it or not, you contribute to your daily happiness. I encourage you to do so consciously and to use that influence beneficially. It's about taking back your power over your happiness. How strongly will you let external circumstances influence the day you will have? Are you going to let others "ruin your day" and have that much control over your mood? Or have you decided to feel good today and make the best of it, whatever it may bring?

Even in tough situations, although hard, often you have a choice in how you want to act, react, and ultimately feel about the situation. That's where resilience comes into play.

You are not a victim of your past, circumstances, pain, mood, or thoughts. Accept that you do have some control over the situation. Maybe you can't change the external situation, but you could change your reaction (=internal situation).

If it's raining, you can't make it stop raining. But you can either be in a bad mood all day or shrug it off, maybe even find advantages of it raining and focus on those. "Hey, I don't have to water the plants in my garden today!" Or: "Yay, perfect weather to watch a movie tonight and enjoy a warm cup of tea." When I was young, we put on our swimsuits and ran around in the rain (in summer). If that's not the ultimate way of making rain fun, I don't know what is!

Do you get where I'm going with this? Most of us don't want to hear it, and many forget it in those moments when it matters. You can remind yourself with post-its or tell your friends to remind you when you're complaining. That won't help, though, if you're not open to it.

How much we complain is also in our power. We all know at least one person who complains endlessly whenever you talk to them. Some always have something new to complain about while others like to complain about the same problem over and over again. Every. Time. You. Meet.

It's exhausting. They suck all the energy out of you, they're an energy vampire. You leave feeling drained. Sometimes I wonder if they leave feeling drained or if my energy has been transferred to them.

Don't get me wrong, a certain amount of complaining is healthy. But I prefer it to be paired with at least a little motivation to improve the situation. I have met quite a few people who refuse to accept or come up with any solutions to their problems. They would rather complain, and no solution or advice you offer is ever good enough to even try out. You've let them vent, and you've been a shoulder to cry on, but eventually, you grow tired of being around that person if they pull you down to their level of negativity.

They may be trapped in a victim mentality, where they feel they have no power or control over the situation. They may feel any attempt to make it better will be in vain. A strong form of helplessness blocks them from advancing out of their problems.

If you are one of those people, I highly encourage you to challenge your thinking. You have a finite amount of energy each day. What are you going to use that for? Complaining or finding and trying out solutions? Which one will get you to where you want to go?

Should you like complaining, then that's okay, too. But be honest with yourself. You owe that to yourself. Do you like being that way, or do you secretly wish it were different? I'm not trying to force you into things you don't want to do. I've come to realize that those thought patterns don't serve me and, frankly, annoy me when others display them.

I've accepted responsibility for my life. For my happiness. I'll be honest, some days that works better than others. But who isn't a work in progress? It's about growth and intention. You need to be self-aware and catch yourself in those moments.

Some people need time to get to that point where they can act and look for a solution rather than admiring the problem. I get that. Let's save us all some time, though, and realize sooner rather than later that this will not get you anywhere worth going.

This mindset of accepting your responsibility for your happiness to a certain extent is the mindset that will help you tackle the new food-allergy challenges more quickly. Yes, you may need to complain and process your feelings (as discussed in the acceptance chapters). But ultimately, to be happy, you will need to *choose* to be happy despite having this allergy. Are you going to let this allergy ruin your mood all your life? I sure hope not.

I want to remind you, you have a choice:
- ♥ To be positive or negative
- ♥ To be grateful for what's going well
- ♥ To be happy
- ♥ To fight or to give up
- ♥ To change what you can't accept and accept what you can't change
- ♥ To put your energy towards looking for solutions, not toward complaining

- ♥ To laugh at crappy situations that didn't go your way or to get mad
- ♥ To blame the world for all they're doing wrong or to lead by example and show the world how to do it right
- ♥ To honk at that guy who just cut you off or to remember that we all make mistakes, we've all been in a hurry, we're all imperfect, and to acknowledge that you don't know his story/reasons for acting the way he did
- ♥ To be mad at that guy that stole your parking spot and then be moody all day or to just drive on and find a new place to park your car
- ♥ To tell yourself, "It's useless, there's nothing I can do," or to ask yourself, "What can I do to make myself feel better right now?"

***

Next, some thoughts on control. With all this talk of accepting responsibility for the things you *can* control, there are things you can't. In those moments, it's helpful to challenge your reaction and thoughts.

I find it hard to let go and relax because I like being in control. I've also noticed how constantly being in control is exhausting and not so much fun. When you control "everything," things will often go your way, which can feel great. But I've found that my environment also adapts, and they lean back a bit. Then I'm forced to be in control all the time, and it feels like a vicious circle. Not always being in control is a normal (and probably healthy) part of life.

I'm a caring person, so I'm always worried about my partner eating healthy and taking a good lunch to work (not because I'm the woman and he's the man, but because I care about food a lot and he doesn't as much). Being the aware individual I am, I realized that my bending over backward, and cooking daily so that there are leftovers for him to take to work, isn't doing us any favors. His lack of accepting responsibility or perhaps my taking on responsibilities that aren't mine has led to frustration and exhaustion. I needed to step back. We talked about it, and we're taking turns cooking now. And yes, sometimes, I need to let him go to work without taking lunch from home. There's only so much I can do.

In these times, there has been one sentence I picked up that never fails to cheer me up in those times: not my circus, not my monkeys. It's a Polish expression and another way of saying "not my problem" or "not my responsibility." Because sometimes, it's not your responsibility. And it's okay to let go.

To see control from another angle, realize that some things happen in life that are out of your control. Pets die. Accidents happen. Someone you love gets sick… As much as we want to prevent this from happening, we need to accept that we can't. There are things you don't have control over. You getting a food allergy, for example.

I used to wonder how all of a sudden, I had an allergy when I didn't before. Or why I had an allergy. Gluten isn't poison to humans in general; other people are eating it and doing just fine. But somehow, my body has declared it as poison (excuse this dramatic way of putting it). I have to accept it and know these things happen in life. Spending my energy on thoughts of "why me" or "why now" is a waste.

In my case, fate struck. My best friend does not have a gluten allergy- it didn't strike her. And that's okay. That's the way life is sometimes. There's nothing I can do about it. So, I accepted it and focused my energy not on fighting it, but on living with it and building a wonderful life despite these circumstances. This revelation has brought me peace of mind and carried me through. Not only regarding my food allergy but also in other difficult situations.

We are as happy as we make our minds up to be, aren't we? I've decided to be happy despite the challenges I face every day.

I will leave you with this, in my eyes, valuable quote. It's Reinhold Niebuhr's Serenity Prayer:

> *God, grant me the serenity to accept the things I cannot change,*
> *courage to change the things I can,*
> *and wisdom to know the difference.*

HEALTHY OPTIMISM AND BEING SOLUTION-DRIVEN

I've already discussed this topic in more detail here and there throughout the book, for example, in the chapter on pain points and finding solutions. Still, I have some thought nudges for you on the topic.

Healthy optimism will get you through many difficulties in life. You don't want that naïve, unrealistic optimism where you shrug everything off, think it will all work itself out, and improve someday. But we are aiming for healthy optimism where you do what you can and hope for the best, but you are prepared to a realistic extent for the worst. It's also about believing in yourself and that you'll make it through whatever happens.

Combined with healthy optimism, I feel being solution-driven makes a difference. Instead of admiring the problem and getting stuck complaining, you are looking for ways to deal with the issue positively and make the best of a situation. It's all about where your focus goes.

For every problem, there's at least one solution. Look for it. Maybe you'll even find multiple solutions. Pick the one you like the most. Then act on it. Remember that acting on it can also mean not actively doing anything. If someone keeps bothering you, a solution could be not to engage in their conversation. You've decided that the best solution for you is to ignore them today, so you act on it by doing nothing.

CONFIDENCE AND BOUNDARIES

You will need a little confidence to get you through. Even if you don't feel confident, I suggest acting the way a confident version of you would. Your body depends on you to stand up for yourself and respect your food allergy.

Whether you like it or not, your body has set a boundary. For me, it's "don't eat gluten." And now, it is up to me to respect and enforce that boundary. This requires confidence and courage. You will see that standing up for your boundaries benefits you in so many areas of life. It's well worth the invested time and energy. Setting boundaries is a whole topic, so further look into it if it interests you. In the network part of this book, I have shown you examples of how you can voice those boundaries and speak up for yourself.

Some people I talked to with a food allergy have feelings of being a burden. That's understandable. Watching how it can negatively affect people's confidence is heartbreaking. I'm not going to sugar-coat it, there may be people who feel that way about you and think you're a burden. Just like some people don't like you for who you are. It's not a great feeling, but you can't be everyone's cup of tea. You probably know people you don't like either.

I want to stress that you have a choice in dealing with this. If someone else doesn't like me, does that mean I have to like myself any less? If someone thinks I'm a burden, should I believe them? Should I care? Try not to let it negatively affect your confidence in yourself.

I see it this way. I want to manage the situation actively. Either by talking about it or limiting my time in their presence. I need to protect myself and know my self-worth.

Depending on who gives me these vibes, I ask myself: can I talk to them about this? Give them the benefit of the doubt that perhaps they're not being sensitive and don't realize how this makes me feel. Also, I try to have constructive conversations with them. Is there a way I can assist them when they are hosting a party and feel overwhelmed/uncertain about how to deal with my allergy?

If they are uncooperative and make me feel like crap, I consider removing myself from their presence when I can. If someone doesn't like me and doesn't treat me well, I don't schedule daily interactions with them so they can bring me down. Instead, I try to minimize my time with them.

Some people, like family or work colleagues, are difficult to avoid. In those scenarios, you will need to prepare yourself. Give yourself a pep talk before interacting with them. Tell yourself that their opinion of you has no value unless you give it one. If someone tells me I'm stupid, I shrug it off. Because

I know I'm not. That comment has no value. The idea is: don't give people the keys to drive you crazy.

If someone tells me I'm making everything more difficult with my food allergy, I know I'm watching out for myself and honoring my body's boundaries. They may never have been in this situation and lack empathy, but I choose not to let it get me down. I bring many things to the table, even if gluten isn't one of them.

PERSPECTIVE AND GRATITUDE

I want to give you a short story to bring my point across. Lisa was born into a poor but loving family. Some days, they had no money for food. But her parents always made her feel loved and cherished. "Man, if my parents had more money and we could eat mac and cheese each day, like Tim, wouldn't that be great?" she thinks.

Tim was born into a rich family where both parents had jobs and little interest in him. They don't have time to cook, so they leave mac and cheese out for Tim daily. He prepares this meal for himself and eats it alone. "Man, if I had someone to eat this mac and cheese with, wouldn't that be nice?" he thinks to himself.

Both Tim and Lisa have something that the other person wants. They also want something the other person has. Often, we don't have everything we want, but we have something someone else wants that we may take for granted.

It's all about perspective. Check your privilege. I know that you have something someone else is wishing for. Be grateful for that. Be creative and look around. What do you have that you wouldn't want to give up? There are so many great things.

Don't wait for your health to be gone to realize its importance. Every day you wake up, be grateful for what you have. If you're in a bad situation, be grateful for your strength and endurance to fight for a better life. Even if you think you don't have enough strength, you do, and you are so, so strong.

As humans, we often get used to what we have and aspire to get something more. These desires have fueled our development over the years and have many advantages. We invented air-conditioning because we don't like it when it's too hot in the summer. If we had always been content with everything the way it is, we might not have invented it.

This pattern of thinking, however, can make us forget how far we've come. We sit in the air-conditioned house and want something more. Wanting more is not bad, but we shouldn't forget to be happy about the air-conditioning sometimes, you know?

Some people keep a gratitude journal. Others wake up and list three things they are grateful for each morning. Some like to list these things at night. Don't wait until Thanksgiving rolls around each year to recognize what you have and are grateful for.

For inspiration, I want to list *some* things I'm grateful for.
- ♥ Having a roof over my head and a bed to sleep in.
- ♥ Getting to eat when I'm hungry and drinking clean water when I'm thirsty.
- ♥ My partner and his love for me.

- ♥ I live in a country where I feel safe.
- ♥ I had the privilege to go to university and study.
- ♥ My desk allows me to adjust its height. That way, I can work either sitting or standing.
- ♥ Lemonade.
- ♥ I experience the sound of the wind blowing through tall trees now and then.
- ♥ I have a job and get paid regularly.
- ♥ I have vacation and get to travel now and then.
- ♥ Pizza.
- ♥ Christmas decoration.
- ♥ Hot chocolate.
- ♥ Snow.
- ♥ My body and that I get to run and do sports.
- ♥ My hair color.
- ♥ Gluten-free options exist.
- ♥ The doctors discovered I had an allergy, so now I can eat how my body needs me to.

When you're making this list, don't forget to *feel* grateful. When I first tried consciously practicing gratitude, I made the lists like everyone said I should. But little changed. It's when I allowed myself to *feel* grateful that it had a noteworthy impact on my life.

Things I'm grateful for:

♥ _____

♥ _____

NOT ALLERGIC TO HAPPINESS, JUST GLUTEN!

♥ _____
♥ _____
♥ _____
♥ _____
♥ _____
♥ _____
♥ _____
♥ _____
♥ _____
♥ _____
♥ _____
♥ _____
♥ _____
♥ _____
♥ _____
♥ _____
♥ _____
♥ _____
♥ _____
♥ _____
♥ _____
♥ _____

FRIENDLY THOUGHTS

For many years, I let my thoughts run free and never examined them closely. Until I realized that I had internalized many other voices that weren't my own so to speak. I wasn't hearing voices or anything. But, for example, there are certain sentences that my parents used to say I had incorporated into my thoughts.

A wonderful but difficult part of growing up is revisiting thoughts and beliefs. Which ones will you keep? Which will you discard or change? If a parent always tells you that you shouldn't relax until all the work is done (or even if they just model that behavior), chances are that's what you'll internalize. Then, one day, you decide whether you want to continue to believe that or whether you think differently.

Additionally, we have different ways of thinking that may or may not be beneficial. In this section, I want to go over some of those with you and give you pointers on ways you can make a positive change.

Before we dive in, though, let me offer advice on how to change your thoughts. I never knew how to go about that because thoughts seem so hard to grasp. And how am I supposed to change them?

Journaling is a great way to revisit your thoughts and analyze them. This need not be in written form. You can also record yourself speaking on an issue that means a lot to you. After you've documented your thoughts, take a break for a day and let it sink in.

Then later, go back to those documents and analyze them. What negative or positive sentences/reactions do you see? Do you want to keep them or change them? Is there anything else you find striking that you'd like to change? Feel free to mark it all in the text or write it down. Then, record yourself speaking about that incident again. Only this time in the way you'd like to think about it or react to these situations.

Another is talking to yourself. Things you mutter under your breath. If I'm driving and someone honks at me, I often say the thought I'd like to think aloud. I could say something like, "honking isn't going to make me any faster, buddy, I'm doing my best," when internally, I may have reacted with a feeling of "oh crap, I have to hurry up, I'm too slow for this world." Over time, those sentences spoken aloud will change your internal dialogue.

Next, you can use your conversations with people to work on your thoughts. Are you venting to someone and catching yourself saying things that no longer serve you? Just call it out. "Actually, let me rephrase that..." and you're good to go.

The last one is more difficult. It's catching yourself in the act while you're thinking. During the day, you can notice what you're thinking and choose to change your thoughts. The cafeteria may serve pizza today, and I may think, "Oh man, why am I missing out on pizza?" I may notice how I am now feeling worse than I was before. I may blame the pizza for triggering me, which may be part of it, but my reactions also play an important role. Having noticed it, I may reframe my thinking to "man, that pizza sure looks good. But I brought this yummy soup with me today; I'm going to enjoy this. Maybe I'll make pizza this weekend."

With these methods, you should be able to change your thoughts bit by bit and make them more friendly. Now we can dive into more specific topics on ways your thoughts may get you down- that you may not have been aware of.

***

Watch Your Language

It's not what you say, it's how you say it. As an impatient, direct person, I sometimes struggle with this. But it's true. When speaking to others, the message they receive from us varies depending on our tone and vocabulary. With yourself, the language you use impacts how you feel and the thoughts that follow afterward as well.

If you're using dramatic words such as always, never, everything, or everyone, chances are you're using language that may tear you down. To catch yourself, look out for these specific categories: extent (everything vs. just this) and timing (forever vs. just for now).

When using these words, an alarm clock should go off in your head. Reflect on how true that sentence is. Is *everything* difficult, or are you going through *something* difficult? This black-or-white thinking and overgeneralization is often very extreme and fuels negative thinking.

When you fail at a new recipe, are you *always* stupid, unable to cook, and your life is now *forever* a failure? Or did you make a mistake and not do it correctly *this time*? There's no need to jump to conclusions or forget about all those times you were good at cooking.

The language you use is powerful regarding the emotions your thoughts produce. Be aware of this and decide whether you would like to change. If you want to change, it may take some time. As mentioned, it can help to speak your thoughts aloud, especially with the new language you want to use. This will help you "train" yourself to express your thoughts differently.

What also helps is thinking of someone who speaks kindly. Do you have someone in your life like that? Or perhaps you've seen them in a movie? In your mind, use their voice or character to speak to yourself kindly. What would that person say to you in this situation? This can help you get a good start when you don't know where to begin. Who knows? You may even keep that persona in your self-talk.

***

Comparisons

I'm sure you've heard something like "comparisons make you unhappy." I want to challenge that. The wrong type of comparison makes you unhappy. Some comparisons, you will find, can even make you happy and grateful for your privilege.

There are two types of comparisons I would like to discuss. The first, I like to call the "better-than-me" comparisons. They are often the most common. To many, these come easily. You compare yourself with people who have it better. Perhaps even more painful, you compare yourself with your past self when *you* had it better.

The second I call the "same-or-worse-than-me" comparisons. Not everyone has it better than you. Many are in similar situations or have it worse. These comparisons can be a way to give yourself some perspective and leave your ego's pity party. But to do that, it's beneficial to investigate the "better-than-me" comparisons because they come quite naturally to most, and we often don't give them a second thought. I invite you to give these a second thought, dig deep, and free yourself from this negative thinking pattern.

"I can't just go out anymore like normal people. I always have to plan everything!" is an example of a "better-than-me" comparison. See how I referred to others as normal in that sentence? Let's talk about that for a second. What is normal anyways? If you define "normal" as the majority of people, then yes, specifically with my gluten allergy, I'm not normal. Most people don't have a gluten allergy.

But still, the dramatic comparison is not quite correct. Many other people have to plan "everything" before going out. What about someone who has (social) anxiety? Who has depression? Who is in a wheelchair? Who is blind? Who has a different type of allergy? Chances are that more people need to plan going out than you might think. No need to single yourself out like that. You are not the only person suffering. And just like that, another type of comparison saved you and gave you a reality check: the "same-or-worse-than-me" comparison.

Don't be afraid to dig deep. With "normal," I was not only referring to others or the ideal healthy person (does that person even exist? And if so, they're very lucky but are they normal?). I was also referring to when it was normal for me to go out and eat anywhere I wanted. The true fight here is accepting my present and future. Not expecting the same life I had before my diagnosis and making the most of what is now a reality.

Life is different now, and it takes some getting used to. You mourn these losses and learn to move on to what is now. What can I do *now* to make my life wonderful- despite everything that's going on? Because there will always be something going on. What can you do? I say you get over yourself, plan something, and go out to see: your life is more normal than you thought it was!

Ultimately, the goal is to spend less time indulging in "better-than-me" comparisons. Over time, you will practice and learn which thoughts are beneficial and which thoughts tear you down. Did you realize that you don't have to follow each thought down the rabbit hole? I took a long time to realize this, but it set me free once I did. You can identify certain thoughts and choose not to follow them. You need time, practice, and a whole lot of patience. The app headspace helped me. If you haven't tried their (guided) meditation before, I recommend you give it a go.

To minimize the "better-than-me" comparisons, it's helpful to examine them closely. Valid feelings are coming up, and you need to process them before you can move on. In my experience, it is not sensible to ignore feelings and hope they go away. Because they won't. They will build up and force you to look at them. If you can, I invite you to look at them sooner rather than later.

You will find that the more "negative" feelings you have processed, the less these "better-than-me" comparisons will occupy your mind. You will notice comparisons coming up, think, "Hey, I've already thought this one through," and let it go down the rabbit hole all by itself. We've already been there and are not in the mood to go there today. We're not going to let this bring us down. Not today!

You may ask: How do I deal with these feelings then? How do I examine these comparisons? To give you some guidance, I have worked out some steps that help me. Try it and adjust it to fit your needs and your style.

Here's a step-to-step guide with nine steps on how to deal with the "better-than-me" comparisons:

1. **Be aware.**
2. **Spot it. Write it down.**
3. **Highlight dramatic language.**

To come back to this example: "I can't just go out anymore like normal people. I always have to plan everything!." Did you notice the "always" and the "everything?" Very dramatic and likely not true. Remember what I mentioned in the "Watch Your Language" section.

4. **Who are you comparing yourself to? What's the situation?**

5. **Dig deep and find your needs.**
Find the underlying wish, hope, fear, or need you have. If you're jealous, what are you jealous of? What do you want?
6. **Process feelings.**
How does this make you feel? Sad, angry, frustrated, hopeless...? Where do you feel this in your body? Breathe and stay with the feeling. Practice self-compassion. Talk to yourself as you would to a friend.

Here are examples:

♥ Sad, grieving:

"It sucks that we can't do that anymore. I totally get it. Go ahead if you need to cry this one out and feel bad for a bit. I'm here, and I'm suffering with you. Let it out. We'll let it rain for a bit."

Then, go get yourself your favorite drink, maybe some tea or hot chocolate, and do what you need at that moment that's light/fun. Either way, reward yourself and be proud!

♥ Mad, angry, frustrated:

"I'm with you on this one. Let's get this anger out in a good way. Want to do some push-ups? Go for a walk or a run? Scream into a pillow or a bowl of water? Listen to loud music? Dance it out? Write your heart out in your journal? Talk to someone about it? Distract yourself?"

Word of caution: avoid driving when you're mad.

♥ Hopeless:

"I know you feel hopeless. But there is hope. Some solutions take more time. Be patient, and keep looking, keep fighting. What you may need now is some rest. You can't fight all the time. Recharge a bit and focus on something else for a change." What's one thing you can do right now to make yourself feel better?

7. **Find ways to meet your needs:**

Are there any solutions you can implement to the issue you uncovered? If, for example, you're mad you can't go to your favorite pizza place anymore, could you try looking for a new favorite pizza place? Is there anything you can or should do for yourself? Don't worry if there isn't. Sometimes feeling and processing emotions was all you needed.

8. **Bonus: identify your triggers.**

Is there one thing (like passing a certain pizza place) that upsets you every time? Knowing this will help you manage your reactions and emotions. Include this in your self-talk if you like; "of course, I'm cranky right now. I just passed Luigi's again."

9. **Be proud of yourself.**

It may not feel like it now, but the weight you're carrying is getting lighter, and you are one step closer to happiness.

You can use comparisons to find your needs, feelings, and triggers. You can also use other "occasions" to implement some of these steps to help you. For example, if you notice a strong emotional reaction that requires some of your love and attention, the steps mentioned above can help you get to the root of it.

***

No Ruminations- You're not a Cow

Did you know that cows are ruminants? The way their digestive system works is that they eat grass, for example, and swallow it. To digest it properly, they regurgitate it and chew it again. Sounds kind of gross, I know.

In psychology, rumination also exists and usually refers to your thoughts. How many times have we had a negative thought and continued to think it until we had let it affect our mood for the whole day?

There is a case for revisiting certain thoughts and processing them. Still, there is also a case for not entertaining the same thoughts again and again without reason. If you spend multiple times a day, week, or year thinking about how you can't have chocolate chip cookie dough ice cream anymore, this probably will not lead you to happiness. These thoughts are not productive unless you find a solution or take action. Usually, they are not doing you any good.

Something I learned from meditation, which was mindblowing for me, was that I did not have to follow every thought. I have a good memory, and I used to believe I could think my way to solutions and feeling better. If I had a thought, I followed that thought 100% of the time to see where it led. Thoughts come up for a reason, don't they?

I did this for years. It took me forever to fall asleep because I was busy sorting my thoughts. I can't sleep when I've got all these thoughts begging me to follow them, can I? It was a workaholic type of behavior. I had too many "thought tabs" open in my "brain browser" and felt like I had to close each tab separately when it would have probably been more advisable to close the browser (including all its tabs) instead.

Enter meditation. I started guided meditation because I was curious. I learned new concepts from the headspace app. Hold on, I can have a thought and let it go? I don't need to relive embarrassing moments that just pop up? If I recognize a negative thought, I can decide to think about something different instead or focus on my breath, and it will go away?

At first, I was skeptical. Is this a good idea? But I was becoming more aware of the thoughts knocking on my door. I noticed that often, I had the same thoughts stopping by. Thoughts I had had before. Thoughts I had followed before. Thoughts that had always led me to the same place and some of which made me very sad or frustrated. I guess it was worth a try.

And so I experimented with that. When I recognized a negative thought that wasn't new, I let it go. I thought of something else or distracted myself. And it was helping me. I looked out for "types" of thoughts. Ones just not helpful for me.

To give you an example, I noticed the "what if" category was generally feeding my anxiety and not helpful. It wasn't the "what if I'm hungry there? I'd better pack some snacks!"-type of practical thought. It was more the "what if my friends secretly think I'm being 'too much' with this allergy and don't like me anymore"-type of thought. Because, really, my friends like me and when they don't anymore, we can either talk about it like adults or the friendship may end. Either way, I'll be okay and cross that bridge when/if I get there.

When those thoughts came, I decided to think of something else or listen to a song I liked. Some days I felt weird like I was ignoring my thoughts and feelings. But on most days, I noticed how much lighter I felt. I gave myself permission to not think too much while trying to fall asleep. The thoughts will still be there in the morning; at that moment, I'm off duty and allowed to rest.

This has been an example of what worked for me. Being aware, open to trying this, and patient was essential. I still don't fall asleep within two minutes, but the nights when I lay in bed for an hour before going to sleep have decreased drastically. Also, it depends on how much I have going on. If I have too many things planned, my increased volume of thoughts lets me know that my stress level is a bit too high.

What's also helped me here is being more open to seeing how things unfold. I don't have to plan everything in advance or be prepared for every situation. For me, rumination was either based on the past (which often made me depressed) or on the future (which made me anxious). I decided to live in the present more and have my thoughts reflect this choice. To have my mind be where my body is.

HUMOR

I imagine this can differ depending on your character or sense of humor. Generally, I have found that humor lightens the mood and brings so much light into a situation. It has the power to make the unbearable bearable somehow. And did you know laughing is generally considered healthy?

When I am grieving, it's hard to find something funny in my story. That's where friends/family/coworkers/people with a good sense of humor can come in to help you. Or perhaps sometimes you need to remind yourself to look for the joke in your situation. This only works to some extent. It's worth remembering this, though.

When I hear stories from or tell stories to other people, I usually find that situations in which you have had hardships or which felt very embarrassing end up being the best stories to laugh about. Suffer now, laugh later. Just something to keep in mind.

DEALING WITH STRESS

You need to learn how to cope with stress. Generally in life, but also in the context of your food allergy, some moments will cause you stress, which may take some energy from you. Also, this food allergy may bring new stressful situations that weren't there before.

It is crucial to learn how to refill your batteries. The energy that goes out has to be smaller than the energy that comes in. Otherwise, what you are doing is not sustainable, and you will ultimately break. It's all about keeping it balanced in the long run.

Recharging your batteries looks different to everyone. Introverts need some time alone to recharge after social interactions. Extroverts need social interactions to feel full of energy again. Some people like to draw or be creative, while others like to go for a run. For some, it's lying on the couch the whole day; for others, it's getting outside and being in nature.

I have a list of things that give me energy. I try to make room for them in my life. If I notice my batteries are close to empty, I look for ways to recharge from that list. Not all ideas on the list work on every occasion. But usually, something on that list will work on that given day.

What about you? Can you list some ways you recharge your batteries? I invite you to write them down now.

I recharge my batteries when...

♥ _____

♥ _____

♥ _____

♥ _____

♥ _____

♥ _____

♥ _____

♥ _____

♥ _____

♥ _____

♥ _____

♥ _____

♥ _____

♥ _____

LIFE HACKS: THINKING IN THE RIGHT DIRECTION

Here are questions and sentences that help me daily.

Questions

I like to use the form of a question to get me thinking and doing so more actively.

What are you focusing on?
Remember: what you focus on grows. You can look at everything going wrong and pick out all the annoying things you dislike about the day. Or you can look at all that's going right and see what's great about today.

What does my energy bank account look like right now?
Are you giving out more energy than you're getting in? Are your numbers red or black? You can spend more energy than

you get back for a while. But eventually, your energy bank account will be empty.

Find ways to fill it up.

Do I choose joy?

Find a joyful way of living. Do it for you and your surroundings.

Does something need more love?

Perhaps your room needs more love. Should you clean it, redecorate or sort things out? Marie Kondo's method is to keep only what sparks joy. I like that idea.

Perhaps you need more love and attention from yourself. Do you want to buy yourself flowers? Make yourself tea? Get something to eat? Shower and do a beauty routine? Find the time to go shopping for a new outfit? Read a good book and relax? Work on that to-do list you've been avoiding? Avoid that to-do list that you've been working on for a while?

What can I do now to make myself happier?

What can *you* do? *Now?*

How will I narrate this?

You get to tell your own story. Do you let this "ruin" your day/week/life? Or do you not give it that power?

Also, feel free to change the way you tell your story. As the narrator of your life, you may have told a story one way and then decided you now see it another way. Give yourself that freedom to rewrite your past in that sense.

For example, maybe you were single for a while and would have narrated it as lonely at the time. And perhaps now you look back at that time and narrate it as learning to live alone and being independent. It doesn't mean you weren't ever lonely, but you may also now be seeing the good as well.

How much time and energy do I want to give this thought?

All I'm saying is there's no need to daydream for hours on end about something that will make you unhappy.

***

Sentences

Other times, I use sentences to get me in the right mindset and help me relax. These sentences help me react more positively.

It do be like that sometimes.[2]
It is what it is.
We'll cross that bridge when we get there.
I can't change anyone else but myself.
I will create my own happiness.

---

[2] Incorrect grammar makes things so much lighter sometimes, don't you think?

Now it's your turn. What are your helpful questions/sentences? Do you have any to add to my list? Do you want to copy some from my list? Feel free, that's what they're there for.

Questions/sentences that redirect my thoughts to get me thinking in the right direction:

♥ _____
♥ _____
♥ _____
♥ _____
♥ _____
♥ _____
♥ _____
♥ _____
♥ _____
♥ _____
♥ _____
♥ _____
♥ _____
♥ _____
♥ _____

FINAL THOUGHTS

I have always found it interesting how some circumstances can change so suddenly while others are slow and require time to settle in. Adhering to a strict gluten-free diet has been one of the sudden changes in my life. Like hitting a wall, I could feel the direct impact and tell you the exact minute everything changed.

Digesting this impact and learning to live with it has been one of the slower processes of life. Like a seed growing into a beautiful flower, it takes time and a lot of love, care, and energy. Every day you look at that growth and see little difference from yesterday.

But then, suddenly, you realize you are looking at a blooming flower when you were looking at dirt just a while ago. In this moment of awareness, you see and admire the progress. You admit to yourself that some beautiful things take time to develop.

I would briefly like to share such a moment of awareness with you.

A few years after my diagnosis, I was planning my vacation. It was after the COVID-19 period, so I hadn't traveled for quite some time. I'm planning a sightseeing vacation that requires detailed planning and an excel sheet (at least it does for me). Traditionally, I always have a column for the day, date, location, drive, activities, and place where I'll sleep.

I notice something is missing this time. Something has changed since I last planned this vacation with this Excel sheet. I add a column called "places to eat" so I can include gluten-free restaurants in my vacation plans.

I smile, knowing I have come a long way since I last used this excel. Knowing this might have gotten me down before, but I am now at peace with it. Knowing I have grown and evolved more than I could have hoped for. Knowing that my life has not always gotten easier, but despite it being a beautiful struggle, I am happy with it anyways.

Because, as it turns out, I am in fact not allergic to happiness. Just gluten.

DID YOU LIKE THIS BOOK?

Thank you for taking the time to read this book.

Before you go, I'd like to ask you for a small favor. I am a self-publisher, so I don't have a big publishing company with a marketing budget supporting me.

If you liked my book, a review would help me out a lot. Or perhaps you know someone who could benefit from reading this book? Why not recommend it to them and spread some joy?

Thanks for considering it!

REFERENCES

Boom, Maike Van Den (2015): *Wo geht's denn hier zum Glück?: Meine Reise durch die 13 glücklichsten Länder der Welt und was wir von ihnen lernen können, 4.*, Frankfurt am Main, Deutschland: FISCHER Krüger.

Ginsburg, Kenneth (2014): *Building Resilience in Children and Teens: Giving Kids Roots and Wings*, Elk Grove Village, USA: American Academy of Pediatrics.

Kondo, Marie (2015): *The Life-Changing Magic of Tidying: The Japanese Art*, London, UK: Vermilion.

Kübler-Ross, Elisabeth (2014): *On Grief and Grieving: Finding the Meaning of Grief Through the Five Stages of Loss*, Reprint, New York, USA: Scribner.

Gürtler, Tobias (2022): Resilienz stärken: Wie Sie Ihre Widerstandsfähigkeit im Job trainieren, [online] https://www.handelsblatt.com/karriere/resilienz-staerken-wie-sie-ihre-belastbarkeit-im-job-trainieren/28295284.html [Accessed 03 October 2022].

Nuber, Ursula (2005): Resilienz: Immun gegen das Schicksal?, in: *Psychologie Heute*, no. 9/2005, [online] https://beratungslehrer-vbn.de/wp-content/uploads/Resilienz-Immun-gegen-das-Schicksal.pdf [Accessed 03 October 2022].

Sicherer, Scott H./Hugh A. Sampson (2014): Food allergy: Epidemiology, pathogenesis, diagnosis, and treatment, in: *Journal of Allergy and Clinical Immunology*, Elsevier BV, vol. 133, no. 2, pp. 291-307.e5, [online] doi:10.1016/j.jaci.2013.11.020.

West, Helen and Northrop, Alyssa (2022): The 8 Most Common Food Allergies, Healthline, [online] https://www.healthline.com/nutrition/common-food-allergies#types-of-food-allergies [Accessed 03 October 2022].

Websites of Celiac Disease Foundations/for Celiac Disease:
Australia: https://www.coeliac.org.au/s/
Canada: https://www.celiac.ca/
New Zeeland: https://coeliac.org.nz/
UK: https://www.coeliac.org.uk
USA: https://celiac.org/

ABOUT THE AUTHOR

Liz is an author, businesswoman and soon-to-be yoga teacher. She holds a master's degree in Business Administration and works a corporate job in digital marketing. She grew up in the USA as well as Germany, where she is currently living.

Having been diagnosed with celiac disease/gluten sensitivity at 26, Liz struggled with its psychological effects on her life. Building on years of research and many practical experiences, she has now found a way to love her life despite her dietary restrictions.

Printed in Dunstable, United Kingdom

65864465R10088